Praise :

uncovered editions
www.uncovered-editions.co.uk

Series editor: Tim Coates
Managing editor: Michele Staple

New titles in the series

Already published

uncovered editions

THE TRIALS OF OSCAR WILDE, 1895

TRANSCRIPT EXCERPTS FROM THE TRIALS AT THE OLD BAILEY, LONDON, DURING APRIL AND MAY 1895

∞⊂∞⊃∞

London: The Stationery Office

ISBN 0 11 702737 5

Excerpts taken from transcripts of the trials conducted at the London Central Criminal Court at the Old Bailey during April and May 1895.

A CIP catalogue record for this book is available from the British Library.

Cover photograph shows Oscar Wilde c. 1885.
© Hulton Archive.

Typeset by J&L Composition Ltd, Filey, North Yorkshire.
Printed in the United Kingdom by The Stationery Office, London.

TJ5588 C20 10/01

CONTENTS

About the series

Uncovered editions are historic official papers which have not previously been available in a popular form, and have been chosen for the quality of their story-telling. Some subjects are familiar, but others are less well known. Each is a moment in history.

About the series editor, Tim Coates

Tim Coates studied at University College, Oxford and at the University of Stirling. After working in the theatre for a number of years, he took up bookselling and became managing director, firstly of Sherratt and Hughes bookshops, and then of Waterstone's. He is known for his support for foreign literature, particularly from the Czech Republic. The idea for *uncovered editions* came while searching through the bookshelves of his late father-in-law, Air Commodore Patrick Cave, OBE. He is married to Bridget Cave, has two sons, and lives in London.

Tim Coates welcomes views and ideas on the *uncovered editions* series. He can be e-mailed at tim.coates@theso.co.uk

Born on 16 October 1854 of professional and literary parents—his father a surgeon and writer, his mother a poet—Oscar Wilde left Ireland in 1874 to study at Magdalen College, Oxford. He won the coveted Newdigate prize for the long poem Ravenna *in 1878, and in the early 1880s his wit and flamboyance helped to establish him in the social and artistic circles of London.*

In 1884 Wilde married Constance Lloyd, the daughter of a prominent Irish barrister, but by the late 1880s he was spending more time in hotels than in the London family home in Tite Street, pursuing an extravagant life-style and his love of "art for art's sake". His only novel, The Picture of Dorian Gray *(1891), understood to be partly autobiographical, gave rise to rumours about his homosexuality. Although some of his plays, beginning with* Lady Windermere's Fan *(1892) and culminating with* The Importance of Being Earnest *(1895), brought a new and much-acclaimed form of comedy to the English theatre, the latter ruthlessly exposing Victorian hypocrisies, Wilde's private life and his flaunting of conventional morality alienated him from many of his peers.*

Finally, his friendship with Lord Alfred Douglas, son of John Sholto Douglas, the Marquess of Queensberry, led to his downfall. Wilde's libel suit against Queensberry backfired and he was charged under Section 11 of the Criminal Law Amendment Act 1885.

Whilst sodomy (or buggery as it was then called) had been a civil offence since 1563—when Henry VIII's Statute of 1533 was reinstated—and was in fact a capital offence in England until 1861, the 1885 Act also made "gross indecencies" punishable as a misdemeanour:

> *Any male person who, in public or private, commits or is party to the commission of, or procures or attempts to procure the commission by any male person of any act of gross indecency with another male person, shall be guilty of a misdemeanour, and being convicted thereof shall be liable at the discretion of the Court to be imprisoned for any term not exceeding two years, with or without hard labour.*

This was the law that was used to convict Oscar Wilde.

PART I

∽∾≎∾∽

BACKGROUND TO THE TRIALS

LETTERS FROM OSCAR WILDE TO LORD ALFRED DOUGLAS

The January and March 1893 letters were both read at the libel trial prosecuted by Wilde: the first was introduced by Wilde's attorney, Sir Edward Clarke, to prevent the defence from presenting it in a more dramatic fashion, the second was read by Defence Attorney Edward Carson during his cross-examination of Wilde. The final letter was written following Wilde's release from prison.

Babbacombe Cliff
January 1893

My Own Boy,

Your sonnet is quite lovely, and it is a marvel that those red rose-leaf lips of yours should be made no less for the madness of music and song than for the madness of kissing. Your slim gilt soul walks between passion and poetry. I know Hyacinthus, whom Apollo loved so madly, was you in Greek days. Why are you alone in London, and when do you go to Salisbury? Do go there to cool your hands in the grey twilight of Gothic things, and come here whenever you like. It is a lovely place and lacks only you; but go to Salisbury first.

Always, with undying love,
Yours,
OSCAR

Savoy Hotel
Victoria Embankment, London
March 1893

Dearest of All Boys,

Your letter was delightful, red and yellow wine to me; but I am sad and out of sorts. Bosie, you must not make scenes with me. They kill me, they wreck the loveliness of life. I cannot see you, so Greek and gracious, distorted with passion. I cannot listen to your curved lips saying hideous things to me. I would sooner be blackmailed by every renter* in London than to have you bitter, unjust, hating ... I must see you soon. You are the divine thing I want, the thing of grace and beauty; but I don't know how to do it. Shall I come to Salisbury? My bill here is £49 for a week. I have also got a new sitting-room over the Thames. Why are you not here, my dear, my wonderful boy? I fear I must leave; no money, no credit, and a heart of lead.

Your own
OSCAR

Rouen
August 1897

My own Darling Boy,
I got your telegram half an hour ago, and just send a line to say that I feel that my only hope of again doing beautiful work in art is being with you. It was not so in the old days, but now it is different, and you can really recreate in me that energy and sense of joyous power on which art depends. Everyone is furious with me for going back to you, but they don't understand us. I feel that it is only with you that I can do anything at all. Do remake my ruined life for me, and then our friendship and love will have a different meaning to the world. I wish that when we met at Rouen we had not

* Slang for male prostitute

parted at all. There are such wide abysses now of space and land between us. But we love each other.

Goodnight, dear. Ever yours,

OSCAR

LORD QUEENSBERRY ON OSCAR WILDE

Although Queensberry was charmed by Wilde when they were introduced in late 1892, by early 1894 he was beginning to demand that his son stop seeing him. Alfred Douglas's telegrammed response to his father's April 1894 letter read: "What a funny little man you are." Queensberry ceased to support his son and took increasingly desperate measures to end the relationship. Thwarted from disrupting the opening night's performance of The Importance of Being Earnest *on 14 February 1895—Wilde, forewarned, had him denied entrance and the theatre surrounded by police—Queensberry left a card with the hall porter at the Albemarle Club in London. When he received this ten days later, Wilde told Douglas: "I don't see anything now but a criminal prosecution. My whole life seems ruined by this man." The libel trial ensued. Queensberry's letter to* The Star *was written on the eve of the first criminal trial of Oscar Wilde.*

Letter to his son, Alfred Douglas

1 April 1894

Alfred,

Your intimacy with this man Wilde must either cease or I will disown you and stop all money supplies. I am not going to try and analyse this intimacy, and I make no charge; but to my mind to pose as a thing is as bad as to be it. With my own eyes I saw you in the most loathsome and disgusting relationship, as expressed by your manner and expression. Never in my experience have I seen such a sight as that in your horrible features. No wonder people are talking as they are. Also I now hear on good authority, but this may be false, that his wife is petitioning to divorce him for sodomy and other crimes. Is this true, or do you not know of it? If I thought the actual thing was true, and it became public property, I should be quite justified in shooting him on sight.

Your disgusted so-called Father,

QUEENSBERRY

Card left at the Albemarle Club

For Oscar Wilde, posing as a somdomite [sic].

Note to Wilde at the close of the libel trial

If the country allows you to leave, all the better for the country; but, if you take my son with you, I will follow you wherever you go and shoot you.

Letter to The Star, 25 April 1895

In my time I have helped to cut up and destroy sharks. I had no sympathy for them, but I may have felt sorry and wished to put them out of their pain as soon as possible. What I did say was that as Mr Wilde now seemed to be on his beam ends and utterly down I did feel sorry for his awful position, and that supposing he was convicted of those loathsome charges brought against him that were I the authority that had to mete out the punishment, I would treat him with all possible consideration as a sexual pervert of an utterly diseased mind, and not as a sane criminal. If this is sympathy, Mr Wilde has it from me to that extent.

QUOTATIONS FROM POEMS BY
LORD ALFRED DOUGLAS

During the first criminal trial, Prosecutor Charles Gill questioned Wilde about two poems written by Alfred Douglas that appeared in the same—the first and last—issue of the Oxford magazine The Chameleon *(December 1894) as Wilde's "Phrases and Philosophies for the Use of the Young". Wilde's explanation of "the love that dare not speak its name"—in the excerpt from* Two Loves—*provided one of the highlights of the trial (see pp. 148–9).*

Two Loves

       ... "Sweet youth,
Tell me why, sad and sighing, thou dost rove
These pleasant realms? I pray thee speak me sooth
What is thy name?" He said, "My name is Love."
Then straight the first did turn himself to me
And cried, "He lieth, for his name is Shame,
But I am Love, and I was wont to be
Alone in this fair garden, till he came
Unasked by night; I am true Love, I fill
The hearts of boy and girl with mutual flame."
Then sighing, said the other, "Have thy will,
I am the love that dare not speak its name."

In Praise of Shame

Last night unto my bed methought there came
Our lady of strange dreams, and from an urn
She poured live fire, so that mine eyes did burn
At the sight of it. Anon the floating fame
Took many shapes, and one cried: "I am Shame
That walks with Love, I am most wise to turn
Cold lips and limbs to fire; therefore discern
And see my loveliness, and praise my name."

And afterwards, in radiant garments dressed
With sound of flutes and laughing of glad lips,
A pomp of all the passions passed along
All the night through; till the white phantom ships
Of dawn sailed in. Whereat I said this song,
"Of all sweet passions Shame is loveliest."

WILDE'S WRITINGS ON TRIAL

In the course of the libel trial prosecuted by Wilde, Defence Attorney Edward Carson asked Wilde in cross-examination about the meaning of two of his writings—"Phrases and Philosophies for the Use of the Young" (1894) and the Preface to The Picture of Dorian Gray *(1891). Wilde's answers, although often flippant, gave an illuminating view of his philosophy of life (see pp. 47–64).*

Phrases and Philosophies for the Use of the Young

The first duty in life is to be as artificial as possible.
What the second duty is no one has as yet discovered.

Wickedness is a myth invented by good people to account for the curious attractiveness of others.

If the poor only had profiles there would be no difficulty in solving the problem of poverty.

Those who see any difference between soul and body have neither.

A really well-made buttonhole is the only link between Art and Nature.

Religions die when they are proved to be true.

Science is the record of dead religions.

The well-bred contradict other people. The wise contradict themselves.

Nothing that actually occurs is of the smallest importance.

Dullness is the coming of age of seriousness.

In all unimportant matters, style, not sincerity is the essential.

In all important matters, style, not sincerity is the essential.

If one tells the truth, one is sure, sooner or later, to be found out.

Pleasure is the only thing one should live for. Nothing ages like happiness.

It is only by not paying one's bills that one can hope to live in the memory of the commercial classes.

No crime is vulgar, but all vulgarity is crime.

Vulgarity is the conduct of others.

Only the shallow know themselves.

Time is a waste of money.

One should always be a little improbable.

There is a fatality about all good resolutions. They are invariably made too soon.

The only way to atone for being occasionally a little overdressed is by being always absolutely over-educated.

To be premature is to be perfect.

Any preoccupation with ideas of what is right or wrong in conduct shows an arrested intellectual development.

Ambition is the last refuge of the failure.

A truth ceases to be true when more than one person believes in it.

In examinations the foolish ask questions that the wise cannot answer.

Greek dress was in its essence inartistic. Nothing should reveal the body but the body.

One should either be a work of art, or wear a work of art.

It is only the superficial qualities that last. Man's deeper nature is soon found out.

Industry is the root of all ugliness.

The ages live in history through their anachronisms.

It is only the gods who taste of death. Apollo has passed away, but Hyacinth, whom men say he slew, lives on.

Nero and Narcissus are always with us.

The old believe everything; the middle-aged suspect everything; the young know everything.

The condition of perfection is idleness; the aim of perfection is youth.

Only the great masters of style ever succeed in being obscure.

There is something tragic about the enormous number of young men there are in England at the present moment who start life with perfect profiles, and end by adopting some useful profession.

To love oneself is the beginning of a life-long romance.

The Preface to The Picture of Dorian Gray

The artist is the creator of beautiful things. To reveal art and conceal the artist is art's aim.

The critic is he who can translate into another manner or a new material his impression of beautiful things.

The highest, as the lowest, form of criticism is a mode of autobiography.

Those who find the ugly meanings in beautiful things are corrupt without being charming. This is a fault.

Those who find beautiful meanings in beautiful things are cultivated. For these there is hope.

They are the elect to whom beautiful things mean only Beauty.

There is no such thing as a moral or an immoral book. Books are well written, or badly written. That is all.

The nineteenth century dislike of Realism is the rage of Caliban seeing his own face in a glass.

The nineteenth century dislike of Romanticism is
the rage of Caliban not seeing his own face in a glass.
The moral life of man forms part of the subject-
matter of the artist, but the morality of art consists in
the perfect use of an imperfect medium. No artist
desires to prove anything.

Even things that are true can be proved.

No artist has ethical sympathies. An ethical sympathy
in an artist is an unpardonable mannerism of style.
No artist is ever morbid. The artist can express
everything.

Thought and language are to the artist instruments of
an art.

Vice and virtue are to the artist materials for an art.
From the point of view of form, the type of all the
arts is the art of the musician. From the point of view
of feeling, the actor's craft is the type.

All art is at once surface and symbol. Those who go
beneath the surface do so at their peril. Those who
read the symbol do so at their peril.

It is the spectator, and not life, that art really mirrors.
Diversity of opinion about a work of art shows that
the work is new, complex, and vital.

When critics disagree the artist is in accord with himself.

We can forgive a man for making a useful thing as
long as he does not admire it. The only excuse for
making a useless thing is that one admires it intensely.
All art is quite useless.

PART II

∞⟨⟩∞

THE LIBEL TRIAL

TRANSCRIPT OF THE LIBEL TRIAL PROSECUTED BY OSCAR WILDE

The libel trial took place at the Old Bailey, 3–5 April 1895. Lord Queensberry pleaded not guilty, claiming that his words were true and that it was for the public benefit that they should be published. Wilde, a few days before the trial—on being urged to flee the country by George Bernard Shaw and Frank Harris—claimed that the charges were absolutely false and groundless. Sir Edward Clarke delivered the prosecution's opening statement and then examined Sidney Wright, the porter at the

*Albemarle Club, and Wilde, but—contrary to expecta-
tions—did not call Lord Alfred Douglas as a witness.
Wilde was questioned on cross-examination by
Queensberry's attorney, Edward Carson, first about his
letters to Douglas and two of his own published works
and then about his past relationships. In his opening
speech for the defence Carson listed who he would be calling as witness the following day.*

OPENING SPEECH FOR THE PROSECUTION

SIR EDWARD CLARKE: May it please you, my lord,
gentlemen of the jury. You have heard the charge
against the defendant, which is that he published a
false and malicious libel in regard to Mr Oscar Wilde.
That libel was published in the form of a card left by
Lord Queensberry at a club to which Mr Oscar
Wilde belonged. It was a visiting card of Lord
Queensberry's, with his name printed upon it, and it
had written upon it certain words which formed the
libel complained of. On that card his lordship wrote:
"Oscar Wilde posing as a sodomite." Of course, it is a
matter of serious moment that such a libel as that
which Lord Queensberry wrote upon that card
should in any way be connected with a gentleman
who has borne a high reputation in this country. The
words of the libel are not directly an accusation of the
gravest of all offences; the suggestion is that there was

no guilt of the actual offence, but that in some way or other the person of whom those words were written did appear—nay, desired to appear—and pose to be a person guilty of or inclined to the commission of the gravest of all offences. You will appreciate that the leaving of such a card openly with the porter of a club is a most serious matter and one likely gravely to affect the position of the person as to whom that injurious suggestion was made. . . .

The defendant has said that the statement is true and that it is for the public benefit that the statement was made, and he has given particulars in the plea of matters which he has alleged show that the statement is true in regard to Mr Oscar Wilde. The plea has not been read to you, gentlemen. There is no allegation in the plea that Mr Oscar Wilde has been guilty of the offence of which I have spoken, but there is a series of accusations in it mentioning the names of persons, and it is said with regard to those persons that Mr Wilde solicited them to commit with him the grave offence, and that he has been guilty with each and all of them of indecent practices. One would gather from the terms of the plea that Mr Wilde has been unsuccessfully soliciting these persons to commit the offence with him, and that, although that offence is not alleged to have been committed, he has been guilty of indecent practices. It is for those who have taken the responsibility of putting into the plea those serious allegations to satisfy you, gentlemen, if they can, by credible witnesses, or evidence which they think worthy of consideration and entitled to belief, that these allegations are true. I can understand how it is that these statements have been put in the form in which they are found, for these people, who may be called upon to sustain these charges, are people who will necessarily have to admit in cross-examination that they themselves have been guilty of the gravest of offences.

Mr Oscar Wilde is a gentleman, 38 years of age, the son of Sir William Wilde, a very distinguished Irish surgeon and oculist, who did great public service as chairman of the Census Committee in Ireland. Mr Oscar Wilde went in the first instance to Trinity College, Dublin, where he greatly distinguished himself for classical knowledge, earning some of the conspicuous rewards which are given to its students by that distinguished University. His father wished him to go to Oxford, and he went to Magdalen College, Oxford, where he had a brilliant career, obtaining the Newdigate Prize for English poetry. After leaving the University he devoted himself to literature in its artistic side. In 1881 he published a volume of poems and wrote essays on artistic and aesthetic subjects. Many years ago he became a very prominent personality, laughed at by some but appreciated by many, representing a form of artistic literature which recommended itself to many of the foremost minds and most cultivated people. In 1884 he had the good fortune to marry a daughter of the late Mr Horace Lloyd, QC, and from that day to the present he has lived with his wife, who has borne him two children, at Tite Street, Chelsea. He is a member of the Albemarle Club.

Among the friends who went to his house in Tite Street was Lord Alfred Douglas, a younger son of Lord Queensberry. In 1891 Lord Alfred Douglas went to Tite Street, being introduced by a friend of Mr Wilde's. From that time Mr Wilde has been a friend of Lord Alfred Douglas and also of his mother, Lady Queensberry, from whom, on her petition, the Marquess has been divorced. He has again and again been a guest at Lady Queensberry's houses at Wokingham and Salisbury, being invited to family parties there. Lord Alfred Douglas has been a welcome guest at Mr Wilde's house, and at Cromer, Goring, Torquay, and Worthing, when Mr and Mrs Wilde were staying there, Lord Alfred Douglas was a frequent and invited visitor. Until 1892 Mr Wilde did not know the defendant with the exception that he met him once about 1881. In November 1892 Mr Wilde and Lord Alfred Douglas were lunching together at the Café Royal in Regent Street. Lord Queensberry came into the room. Mr Wilde was aware that, owing to circumstances with which he had nothing to do—owing to unhappy family troubles which I only mention because it is absolutely necessary—there had been some strained feelings between Lord Alfred

Douglas and his father. Mr Wilde suggested to Lord
Alfred Douglas that it was a good opportunity for
him to speak to his father and for a friendly interview. Lord Alfred Douglas acted on the suggestion
and went across to Lord Queensberry and spoke to
him and had a friendly conversation. Lord Alfred
Douglas brought Lord Queensberry to the table
where he and Mr Wilde sat at lunch, and Lord
Queensberry was introduced to Mr Wilde and
shook hands with him. Lord Queensberry
reminded Mr Wilde of the fact that 12 years before
they had met at the house of a friend of both of
them. Lord Queensberry sat down and had lunch
with the two men. Lord Alfred Douglas was
obliged to leave about 2.30 p.m. and Lord
Queensberry remained chatting with Mr Wilde.
Mr Wilde said that he and his family were going to
Torquay. Lord Queensberry said that he was going
to Torquay, too, to give a lecture, and asked Mr
Wilde to come and hear it.

Lord Queensberry did not go to Torquay, and
he sent a note to Mr Wilde telling him he was not
going there. Mr Wilde never met Lord
Queensberry from that time until the early part of
1894.

Between that time and 1894, Mr Wilde became
aware that certain statements were being made
against his character—I do not mean by Lord
Queensberry. He became aware of it in this way.
There was a man named Alfred Wood, whom Mr

Wilde had seen once or twice but knew very little indeed about. Wood had been given some clothes by Lord Alfred Douglas, and he stated that in the pocket of a coat so given to him he had found four letters which had been written by Mr Wilde to Lord Alfred. Whether he did find them in the pocket, or whether he stole them, is a matter on which we can only speculate. But, at all events, Wood went to Mr Wilde early in 1893 and wanted Mr Wilde to give him something for the letters, representing that he was in great distress and trouble and wanted to get off to America. Mr Wilde gave him £15 or £20 wherewith to pay his passage. Wood then handed over three very ordinary letters which Mr Wilde had written to Lord Alfred Douglas. But, as generally happens when people think they have got hold of letters of some importance, the letters of no importance were given up, and that which was supposed to be of some importance was retained. That was the case in this instance. The people taking part in these transactions were men named Wood, Allen and Cliburn, and something has been found out about this set of people.

Now, in 1893, Mr Wilde wrote a play, which afterwards proved a great success at the Haymarket Theatre, *A Woman of No Importance*, and while this play was being prepared for production, there came into the hands of Mr Beerbohm Tree, the manager of that theatre, a piece of paper which purported to

be, and to some extent was, a copy of a letter which
had been retained by the persons I have named
when the other letters were handed over. On this
paper was written, "Kindly give this to Mr Oscar
Wilde and oblige yours", and then there followed
some initials. Shortly afterwards Allen called on Mr
Wilde and said he had the original letter. He asked
Mr Wilde to give him something for it. Mr Wilde
absolutely and peremptorily refused, saying: "I have
a copy of that letter and the original is no use to
me. I look upon it as a work of art. I should have
desired to possess it; but, now that you have been
good enough to send me a copy, I do not want the
original." He then sent Allen away, giving him ten
shillings for himself. Almost immediately afterwards
Cliburn came to Mr Wilde and said that Allen had
appreciated Mr Wilde's kindness so much that he
sent back the letter. The man then handed over the
letter, and Mr Wilde gave him half a sovereign for
his trouble.

Having once got the original letter into his
possession, Mr Wilde kept it. Now, here is the letter itself:

My Own Boy,
Your sonnet is quite lovely, and it is a marvel that
those red rose-leaf lips of yours should have been
made no less for music of song than for madness of
kisses. Your slim gilt soul walks between passion and
poetry. I know Hyacinthus, whom Apollo loved so

madly, was you in Greek days. Why are you alone in London, and when do you go to Salisbury? Do go there to cool your hands in the grey twilight of Gothic things, and come here whenever you like. It is a lovely place and lacks only you; but go to Salisbury first. Always, with undying love,

Yours,

OSCAR

The words of that letter, gentlemen, may appear extravagant to those in the habit of writing commercial correspondence—[Laughter]—or those ordinary letters which the necessities of life force upon one every day; but Mr Wilde is a poet, and the letter is considered by him as a prose sonnet, and one of which he is in no way ashamed and is prepared to produce anywhere as the expression of true poetic feeling, and with no relation whatever to the hateful and repulsive suggestions put to it in the plea in this case.

In the early part of 1894 Lord Queensberry met Mr Wilde and Lord Alfred Douglas again at the Café Royal. Shortly after that Mr Wilde became aware that the defendant was writing letters that affected his character and contained suggestions injurious to him. Though he might reasonably— and would probably if his own interests alone were concerned—have brought this to some public notice, he abstained from doing so for reasons which I am not entitled to state, but which I am sure will be obvious before this case has gone very far. And so the latter part of 1894 passed. At an interview in that year, Mr Wilde gave instructions, in Lord Queensberry's hearing, that the defendant should not be admitted into his house.

Last February another play by Mr Oscar Wilde, *The Importance of Being Earnest*, was about to be produced at the St James's Theatre. In the course of the day—14 February—information reached the management of the theatre, and other persons, with regard to certain intentions on the part of Lord Queensberry. It is a matter of public dramatic history that at a play written by the late poet laureate, Lord Tennyson, *The Promise of May*, Lord Queensberry made some observations in the public theatre.

MR EDWARD CARSON: I do not see how this is evidence.

MR JUSTICE COLLINS: It might be pertinent as explaining the extravagant actions of Mr Wilde towards Lord Queensberry.

CLARKE: On that occasion Lord Queensberry got up in the theatre and, in his character as an agnostic, objected to the representation being put upon the stage of an agnostic in the person of Mr Hermann Vezin. He denounced this character from his seat in the stalls. Of course, a disturbance on the night of the production of a new play is a very serious matter to author and actors, and it would have been especially serious if—as it probably would—it had developed into a personal attack on the private character of Mr Wilde. Lord Queensberry booked a seat at the St James's Theatre, but his money was returned to him and the police were warned about him. Lord Queensberry made his appearance in the course of the evening and brought with him a large bouquet made of vegetables.—[Laughter]—Whether Lord Queensberry was responsible for his actions is a matter on which you, gentlemen of the jury, may have some doubts before this case has ended. Instead of writing to the committee of one of the clubs of which Mr Wilde was a member, and asking for an inquiry, he got a bunch of vegetables and came down to the theatre on the first night of Mr Wilde's new play. Being refused admission at the box office, he made his way to the gallery stairs; but here, too, the police had received notice, and being unable to get admission Lord Queensberry went away.

On 28 February Mr Wilde went to the Albemarle Club and there received from the porter the card left by Lord Queensberry on the 18th of that month. . . . On 1 March a warrant was applied for, and on the following day Lord Queensberry was arrested. Hence these criminal proceedings.

There are two counts at the end of the plea which are extremely curious. It is said that [in 1981] Mr Wilde published, or caused to be published, with his name on the title page, a certain immoral and indecent work with the title of *The Picture of Dorian Gray*, which book was intended to be understood by the readers to describe the relations, intimacies and passions of certain persons guilty of unnatural practices. And, secondly, that in December 1894 was published a certain immoral work in the form of *The Chameleon*, relating to the practices of persons of unnatural habits; and that Mr Wilde had joined in procuring the publication of *The Chameleon*, with his name on it, as the principal contributor, under the title of "Phrases and Philosophies for the Use of the Young". Those are two very gross allegations. I defy my learned friend to suggest from these contributions anything hostile to the character of Mr Wilde. *The Chameleon* was numbered Volume I, Number 1; it was published by Messrs Gay & Bird, of 5 Chandos Street; and only 100 copies were to be printed. Mr Wilde did contribute "Phrases and Philosophies for the Use of the Young", and on the first three pages there is a certain number of epigrammatical statements such as those which many of us have enjoyed when being entertained by such a play as *A Woman of No Importance*. They give brilliancy and effect to dialogue and they even supply wisdom in a witty form.

Mr Wilde is not responsible for the rest of the magazine. It was edited by an Oxford man who asked Mr Wilde to contribute. Directly Mr Wilde saw the magazine he noticed there was a story in it called "The Priest and the Acolyte", which is a disgrace to literature, which it is amazing that anybody wrote and still more amazing that anybody allowed to be published under his name. Directly Mr Wilde saw that disgraceful and abominable story he communicated with the editor; he indignantly insisted on the copies being suppressed and the magazine was withdrawn. It is strange indeed, then, to find that publication put upon the particulars as justifying the charge against Mr Wilde.

The volume called *The Picture of Dorian Gray* is one which can be bought at any bookstall in London. It has Mr Wilde's name on the title page and has been published five years. The story of the book is that of a young man of good birth, great wealth and great personal beauty, whose friend paints a picture of him. Dorian Gray expresses the wish that he could remain as in the picture, while the picture aged with the years. His wish is granted, and he soon knows that upon the picture, and not upon his own face, the scars of trouble and bad conduct are falling. In the end he stabs the picture and falls dead, and the picture is restored to its pristine beauty, while his friends find on the floor the body of a hideous old man. I shall be surprised if my learned friend can pitch upon any passage in that book which does more than describe as novelists and dramatists may—nay, must—describe the passions and fashions of life.

Witnesses will be called who will prove the publication of the libel, and my learned friend has the task of satisfying you that the excuses made are true.

TESTIMONY OF SIDNEY WRIGHT, PORTER AT THE ALBEMARLE CLUB

WRIGHT: I am hall porter at the Albemarle Club. Mr and Mrs Oscar Wilde are members of the club. On 18 February the Marquess of Queensberry handed me a card which has been produced. Before handing me the card Lord Queensberry wrote some words on it. Lord Queensberry said he wished me to give that to Mr Wilde. I looked at the card but did not understand it. I made an entry on the back of it of the date and the time at which it was handed to me. I put it in an envelope which I addressed "Mr Oscar Wilde". When Mr Oscar Wilde came to the club, on 28 February, I handed it to him, saying that Lord Queensberry wished me to give it to Mr Wilde.

TESTIMONY OF OSCAR WILDE ON DIRECT EXAMINATION

WILDE: I am the prosecutor in this case. I am 39 years of age. My father was Sir William Wilde, surgeon, of Dublin, and chairman of the Census Commission. He died when I was at Oxford in 1876. I was a student at Trinity College, where I took a classical scholarship and the gold medal for Greek. I then went to Magdalen College, Oxford, where I took a classical scholarship, a first in "Mods", and a first in "Greats", and the Newdigate Prize for English verse. I took my degree in 1878, and came down at once. From that time I have devoted myself to art and literature. In 1881 I published a volume of poems, and afterwards lectured in England and America. In 1884 I married Miss Lloyd, and from that date till now have lived with her in Tite Street, Chelsea. I have two sons, the elder of whom will be ten in June and the second nine in November.

CLARKE: In 1891 did you make the acquaintance of Lord Alfred Douglas?

WILDE: Yes; he was brought to my house by a friend. Before then I had been acquainted with Lady Queensberry, but since then I have been a guest in her house many times. I also knew Lord Douglas of Hawick and the late Lord Drumlanrig. Lord Alfred has dined with me from time to time at my house and at the Albemarle Club, of which my wife is a member, and has stayed with us at Cromer, Goring, Worthing and Torquay. In November 1892 I was lunching with him at the Café Royal, where we met Lord Queensberry, and on my suggestion Lord Alfred went up to him and shook hands. I was aware that there had been some estrangement between the two. Lord Queensberry joined us. Lord Alfred had to go away early, and Lord Queensberry remained and chatted with me. Afterwards something was said about Torquay, and it was arranged that Lord Queensberry should call upon me there, but he did not come. From 3 November 1892 till March 1894, I did not see the defendant, but in 1893 I heard that some letters which I had addressed to Lord Alfred Douglas had come into the hands of certain persons.

CLARKE: Did anyone say that he had found letters of yours?

WILDE: Yes. A man named Wood saw me at the rooms of Mr Alfred Taylor and told me that he had found some letters in a suit of clothes which Lord Alfred Douglas had been good enough to give him.

CLARKE: Did he ask for anything?

WILDE: I don't think he made a direct demand.

CLARKE: What happened?

WILDE: When he entered the room he said: "I suppose you will think very badly of me." I replied: "I hear that you have letters of mine to Lord Alfred Douglas which you certainly ought to have given back." He handed me three or four letters, and said they had been stolen from him "the day before yesterday" by a man named Allen, and that he [Wood] had had to employ a detective to get them back. I read the letters, and said that I did not think them of any importance. He said: "I am very much afraid of staying in London, as this man and other men are threatening me. I want money to go away to America." I asked what better opening as a clerk he could have in America than in England, and he replied that he was anxious to get out of London in order to escape from the man who had taken the letters from him. He made a very strong appeal to me. He said that he could find nothing to do in London. I paid him £15. The letters remained in my hand all the time.

CLARKE: Did some man shortly afterwards come with another letter?

WILDE: A man called and told me that the letter, a copy of which had been sent to Mr Beerbohm Tree, was not in his possession. His name was Allen.

CLARKE: What happened at that interview?

WILDE: I felt that this was the man who wanted money from me. I said: "I suppose you have come about my beautiful letter to Lord Alfred Douglas. If you had not been so foolish as to send a copy of it to Mr Beerbohm Tree, I would gladly have paid you a very large sum of money for the letter, as I consider it to be a work of art." He said: "A very curious construction can be put on that letter." I said in reply: "Art is rarely intelligible to the criminal classes." He said: "A man offered me £60 for it." I said to him: "If you take my advice you will go to that man and sell my letter to him for £60. I myself have never received so large a sum for any prose work of that length; but I am glad to find that there is someone in England who considers a letter of mine worth £60." He was somewhat taken aback by my manner, perhaps, and said: "The man is out of town." I replied: "He is sure to come back", and I advised him to get the £60.

He then changed his manner a little, saying that he had not a single penny, and that he had been on many occasions trying to find me. I said that I could not guarantee his cab expenses, but that I would gladly give him half a sovereign. He took the money and went away.

CLARKE: Was anything said about a sonnet?

WILDE: Yes. I said: "The letter, which is a prose poem, will shortly be published in sonnet form in a delightful magazine and I will send you a copy of it."

CLARKE: Did Allen then go away?

WILDE: Yes, and in about five minutes Cliburn came to the house. I went out to him and said: "I cannot bother any more about this matter." He produced the letter out of his pocket, saying: "Allen has asked me to give it back to you." I did not take it immediately, but asked: "Why does Allen give me back this letter?" He said: "Well, he says that you were kind to him, and that there is no use trying to 'rent' you as you only laugh at us." I took the letter and said: "I will accept it back, and you can thank Allen from me for all the anxiety he has shown about it." I looked at the letter, and saw that it was extremely soiled. I said to him: "I think it is quite unpardonable that better care was not taken of this original manuscript of mine."—[Laughter]—He said he was very sorry, but it had been in so many hands. I gave him half a sovereign for his trouble and then said: "I am afraid you are leading a won-derfully wicked life." He said: "There is good and bad in every one of us." I told him he was a born philosopher, and he then left.

CLARKE: Has the letter remained in your posses-sion ever since?

WILDE: Yes. I produce it here today.

CLARKE: I pass to the end of 1893. Did Lord Alfred Douglas go to Cairo then?

WILDE: Yes; in December 1893.

CLARKE: On his return were you lunching together in the Café Royal when Lord Queensberry came in?

WILDE: Yes. He shook hands and joined us, and we chatted on perfectly friendly terms about Egypt and various other subjects.

CLARKE: Shortly after that meeting did you become aware that he was making suggestions with regard to your character and behaviour?

WILDE: Yes. Those suggestions were not contained in letters to me. At the end of June 1894 there was an interview between Lord Queensberry and myself in my house. He called upon me, not by appointment, about 4 p.m., accompanied by a gentleman with whom I was not acquainted. The interview took place in my library. Lord Queensberry was standing by the window. I walked over to the fireplace, and he said to me: "Sit down." I said to him: "I do not allow anyone to talk like that to me in my house or anywhere else. I suppose you have come to apologise for the statement you made about my wife and myself in letters you wrote to your son. I should have the right any day I chose to prosecute you for writing such a letter."

He said: "The letter was privileged, as it was written to my son." I said: "How dare you say such things to me about your son and me?" He said: "You were both kicked out of the Savoy Hotel at a moment's notice for your disgusting conduct." I said: "That is a lie." He said: "You have taken furnished rooms for him in Piccadilly." I said: "Somebody has been telling you an absurd set of lies about your son and me. I have not done anything of the kind." He said: "I hear you were thoroughly well blackmailed for a disgusting letter you wrote to my son." I said: "The letter was a beautiful letter, and I never write except for publication." Then I asked: "Lord Queensberry, do you seriously accuse your son and me of improper conduct?" He said: "I do not say that you are it, but you look it ..."—[Laughter]—

MR JUSTICE COLLINS: I shall have the Court cleared if I hear the slightest disturbance again.

WILDE: "but you look it, and you pose as it, which is just as bad. If I catch you and my son together again in any public restaurant I will thrash you." I said: "I do not know what the Queensberry rules are, but the Oscar Wilde rule is to shoot at sight." I then told Lord Queensberry to leave my house. He said he would not do so. I told him that I would have him put out by the police. He said: "It is a disgusting scandal." I said: "If it be so, you are the author of the scandal, and no one else." I then went into the hall and pointed him out to my servant. I said: "This is the Marquess of Queensberry, the most infamous brute in London. You are never to allow him to enter my house again." It is not true that I was expelled from the Savoy Hotel at any time. Neither is it true that I took rooms in Piccadilly for Lord Queensberry's son. I was at the theatre on the opening night of the play *The Importance of Being Earnest* and was called before the curtain. The play was successful. Lord Queensberry did not obtain admission to the theatre. I was acquainted with the fact that Lord Queensberry had brought a bunch of vegetables with him.

CLARKE: When was it you heard the first statement affecting your character?

WILDE: I had seen communications from Lord Queensberry, not to his son, but to a third party— members of his own and of his wife's families. I went to the Albemarle Club on 28 February and received from the porter the card which has been produced. A warrant was issued on the 1st of March.

CLARKE: It is suggested that you are responsible for the publication of the magazine *The Chameleon*, on the front page of which some aphorisms of yours appear. Beyond sending that contribution, had you anything to do with the preparation or publication of that magazine?

WILDE: No; nothing whatever.

CLARKE: Until you saw this number of *The Chameleon*, did you know anything about the story "The Priest and the Acolyte"?

WILDE: Nothing at all.

CLARKE: Upon seeing that story in print, did you communicate with the editor?

WILDE: The editor came to see me at the Café Royal to speak to me about it.

CLARKE: Did you approve of the story of "The Priest and the Acolyte"?

WILDE: I thought it bad and indecent, and I strongly disapproved of it.

CLARKE: Was that disapproval expressed to the editor?

WILDE: Yes.

CLARKE: The other question relates to the book *The Picture of Dorian Gray.* Was that first published in serial form?

WILDE: It was first published in Lippincott's, and afterwards in book form with some additional chapters. It was much reviewed.

CLARKE: Your attention has been called to the statements which are made in the pleadings referring to different persons and impugning your conduct with them?

WILDE: Yes.

CLARKE: Is there any truth in any of these accusations?

WILDE: There is no truth whatever in any one of them.

TESTIMONY OF OSCAR WILDE ON CROSS-EXAMINATION

Literary part

MR EDWARD CARSON: You stated that your age was 39. I think you are over 40. You were born on 16 October 1854?

WILDE: I have no wish to pose as being young. I am 39 or 40. You have my certificate and that settles the matter.

CARSON: But being born in 1854 makes you more than 40?

WILDE: Ah! Very well.

CARSON: What age is Lord Alfred Douglas?

WILDE: Lord Alfred Douglas is about 24, and was between 20 and 21 years of age when I first knew him. Down to the time of the interview in Tite Street, Lord Queensberry was friendly. I did not receive a letter on 3 April in which Lord Queensberry desired that my acquaintance with his son should cease. After the interview I had no doubt that such was Lord Queensberry's desire. Notwithstanding Lord Queensberry's protest, my intimacy with Lord Alfred Douglas has continued down to the present moment.

CARSON: You have stayed with him at many places?

WILDE: Yes.

CARSON: At Oxford? Brighton on several occasions? Worthing?

WILDE: Yes.

CARSON: And in various hotels in London?

WILDE: Yes; at one in Albemarle Street, and in Dover Street and at the Savoy.

CARSON: Did you ever take rooms yourself in addition to your house in Tite Street?

WILDE: Yes; at 10 and 11 St James's Place. I kept the rooms from the month of October 1893 to the end of March 1894. Lord Alfred Douglas has stayed in those chambers, which are not far from Piccadilly. I have been abroad with him several times and even lately to Monte Carlo. With reference to the writings which have been mentioned, it was not at Brighton, in 20 King's Road, that I wrote my article for *The Chameleon*. I observed that there were also contributions from Lord Alfred Douglas, but these were not written at Brighton. I have seen them. I thought them exceedingly beautiful poems. One was *In Praise of Shame* and the other *Two Loves*.

CARSON: These loves. They were two boys?

WILDE: Yes.

CARSON: One boy calls his love "true Love", and the other boy calls his love "Shame"?

WILDE: Yes.

CARSON: Did you think that made any improper suggestion?

WILDE: No, none whatever.

CARSON: You read "The Priest and the Acolyte"?

WILDE: Yes.

CARSON: You have no doubt whatever that that was an improper story?

WILDE: From the literary point of view it was highly improper. It is impossible for a man of literature to judge it otherwise; by literature, meaning treatment, selection of subject and the like. I thought the treatment rotten and the subject rotten.

CARSON: You are of opinion, I believe, that there is no such thing as an immoral book?

WILDE: Yes.

CARSON: May I take it that you think "The Priest and the Acolyte" was not immoral?

WILDE: It was worse; it was badly written.

CARSON: Was not the story that of a priest who fell in love with a boy who served him at the altar, and was discovered by the rector in the priest's room, and a scandal arose?

WILDE: I have read it only once, in last November, and nothing will induce me to read it again. I don't care for it. It doesn't interest me.

CARSON: Do you think the story blasphemous?

WILDE: I think it violated every artistic canon of beauty.

CARSON: I wish to know whether you thought the story blasphemous?

WILDE: The story filled me with disgust. The end was wrong.

CARSON: Answer the question, sir. Did you or did you not consider the story blasphemous?

WILDE: I thought it disgusting.

CARSON: I am satisfied with that. You know that when the priest in the story administers poison to the boy, he uses the words of the sacrament of the Church of England?

WILDE: That I entirely forgot.

CARSON: Do you consider that blasphemous?

WILDE: I think it is horrible. "Blasphemous" is not a word of mine.

CARSON [reading from "The Priest and the Acolyte"]:

> Just before the consecration the priest took a tiny phial from the pocket of his cassock, blessed it and poured the contents into the chalice.
>
> When the time came for him to receive from the chalice, he raised it to his lips, but did not taste of it.
>
> He administered the sacred wafer to the child, and then he took his hand; he turned towards him; but when he saw the light in the beautiful face he turned again to the crucifix with a low moan. For one instant his courage failed him; then he turned to the little fellow again, and held the chalice to his lips:
>
> "The Blood of our Lord Jesus Christ, which was shed for thee, preserve thy body and soul unto everlasting life."

CARSON: Do you approve of those words?

WILDE: I think them disgusting, perfect twaddle. ... I strongly objected to the whole story. I took no steps to express disapproval of *The Chameleon* because I think it would have been beneath my dignity as a man of letters to associate myself with an Oxford undergraduate's productions. I am aware that the magazine may have been circulated among the undergraduates of Oxford. I do not believe that any book or work of art ever had any effect whatever on morality.

CARSON: Am I right in saying that you do not consider the effect in creating morality or immorality?

WILDE: Certainly, I do not.

CARSON: So far as your works are concerned, you pose as not being concerned about morality or immorality?

WILDE: I do not know whether you use the word "pose" in any particular sense.

CARSON: It is a favourite word of your own?

WILDE: Is it? I have no pose in this matter. In writing a play or a book, I am concerned entirely with literature—that is, with art. I aim not at doing good or evil, but in trying to make a thing that will have some quality of beauty.

CARSON: Listen, sir. Here is one of the "Phrases and Philosophies for the Use of the Young" which you contributed: "Wickedness is a myth invented by good people to account for the curious attractiveness of others." You think that true?

WILDE: I rarely think that anything I write is true.

CARSON: Did you say "rarely"?

WILDE: I said "rarely". I might have said "never"—not true in the actual sense of the word.

CARSON: "Religions die when they are proved to be true." Is that true?

WILDE: Yes; I hold that. It is a suggestion towards a philosophy of the absorption of religions by science, but it is too big a question to go into now.

CARSON: Do you think that was a safe axiom to put forward for the philosophy of the young?

WILDE: Most stimulating.

CARSON: "If one tells the truth, one is sure, sooner or later, to be found out"?

WILDE: That is a pleasing paradox, but I do not set very high store on it as an axiom.

CARSON: Is it good for the young?

WILDE: Anything is good that stimulates thought in whatever age.

CARSON: Whether moral or immoral?

WILDE: There is no such thing as morality or immorality in thought. There is immoral emotion.

CARSON: "Pleasure is the only thing one should live for"?

WILDE: I think that the realisation of oneself is the prime aim of life, and to realise oneself through pleasure is finer than to do so through pain. I am, on that point, entirely on the side of the ancients— the Greeks. It is a pagan idea.

CARSON: "A truth ceases to be true when more than one person believes in it"?

WILDE: Perfectly. That would be my metaphysical definition of truth; something so personal that the same truth could never be appreciated by two minds.

CARSON: "The condition of perfection is idleness; the aim of perfection is youth"?

WILDE: Oh, yes; I think so. Half of it is true. The life of contemplation is the highest life, and so recognised by the philosopher.

CARSON: "There is something tragic about the enormous number of young men there are in England at the present moment who start life with perfect profiles, and end by adopting some useful profession"?

WILDE: I should think that the young have enough sense of humour.

CARSON: You think that is humorous?

WILDE: I think it is an amusing paradox, an amusing play on words. . . .

CARSON: This is in your introduction to *Dorian Gray*: "There is no such thing as a moral or an immoral book. Books are well written, or badly written." That expresses your view?

WILDE: My view on art, yes.

CARSON: Then, I take it, that no matter how immoral a book may be, if it is well written, it is, in your opinion, a good book?

WILDE: Yes, if it were well written so as to produce a sense of beauty, which is the highest sense of which a human being can be capable. If it were badly written, it would produce a sense of disgust.

CARSON: Then a well-written book putting forward perverted moral views may be a good book?

WILDE: No work of art ever puts forward views. Views belong to people who are not artists.

CARSON: A perverted novel might be a good book?

WILDE: I don't know what you mean by a "perverted" novel.

CARSON: Then I will suggest *Dorian Gray* as open to the interpretation of being such a novel?

WILDE: That could only be to brutes and illiterates. The views of Philistines on art are incalculably stupid.

CARSON: An illiterate person reading *Dorian Gray* might consider it such a novel?

WILDE: The views of illiterates on art are unaccountable. I am concerned only with my view of art. I don't care twopence what other people think of it.

CARSON: The majority of persons would come under your definition of Philistines and illiterates?

WILDE: I have found wonderful exceptions.

CARSON: Do you think that the majority of people live up to the position you are giving us?

WILDE: I am afraid they are not cultivated enough.

CARSON: Not cultivated enough to draw the distinction between a good book and a bad book?

WILDE: Certainly not.

CARSON: The affection and love of the artist of *Dorian Gray* might lead an ordinary individual to believe that it might have a certain tendency?

WILDE: I have no knowledge of the views of ordinary individuals.

CARSON: You did not prevent the ordinary individual from buying your book?

WILDE: I have never discouraged him.

CARSON [reading from *The Picture of Dorian Gray*, in which the painter Basil Hallward describes to Lord Henry Wooton his first meetings with Dorian Gray]:

> "The story is simply this. Two months ago I went to
> a crush at Lady Brandon's. You know we poor
> painters have to show ourselves in society from time
> to time, just to remind the public that we are not
> Savages. With an evening coat and a white tie, as you
> told me once, anybody, even a stockbroker, can gain a

reputation for being civilised. Well, after I had been in the room about ten minutes, talking to huge overdressed dowagers and tedious Academicians, I suddenly became conscious that someone was looking at me. I turned half-way round, and saw Dorian Gray for the first time. When our eyes met, I felt that I was growing pale. A curious instinct of terror came over me. I knew that I had come face to face with someone whose mere personality was so fascinating that, if I allowed it to do so, it would absorb my whole nature, my whole soul, my very art itself. I did not want any external influence in my life. You know yourself, Harry, how independent I am by nature. My father destined me for the army. I insisted on going to Oxford. Then he made me enter my name at the Middle Temple. Before I had eaten half a dozen dinners I gave up the Bar, and announced my intention of becoming a painter. I have always been my own master; had at least always been so, till I met Dorian Gray. Then—but I don't know how to explain it to you. Something seemed to tell me that I was on the verge of a terrible crisis in my life. I had a strange feeling that Fate had in store for me exquisite joys and exquisite sorrows. I knew that if I spoke to Dorian I would become absolutely devoted to him, and that I ought not to speak to him. I grew afraid, and turned to quit the room. It was not conscience that made me do so: it was cowardice. I take no credit to myself for trying to escape."

"Conscience and cowardice are really the same things, Basil. Conscience is the trade-name of the firm. That is all."

"I don't believe that, Harry. However, whatever was my motive—and it may have been pride, for I used to be very proud—I certainly struggled to the door. There, of course, I stumbled against Lady Brandon. 'You are not going to run away so soon, Mr Hallward?' she screamed out. You know her shrill horrid voice?"

"Yes, she is a peacock in everything but beauty," said Lord Henry, pulling the daisy to bits with his long, nervous fingers.

"I could not get rid of her. She brought me up to Royalties, and people with Stars and Garters, and elderly ladies with gigantic tiaras and hooked noses. She spoke of me as her dearest friend. I had only met her once before, but she took it into her head to lionise me. I believe some picture of mine had made a great success at the time, at least had been chattered about in the penny newspapers, which is the nineteenth-century standard of immortality. Suddenly I found myself face to face with the young man whose personality had so strangely stirred me. We were quite close, almost touching. Our eyes met again. It was mad of me, but I asked Lady Brandon to introduce me to him. Perhaps it was not so mad, after all. It was simply inevitable. We would have spoken to each other without introduction. I am sure of that. Dorian told me so afterwards. He, too, felt that we were destined to know each other."

"Tell me more about Dorian Gray. How often do you see him?"

"Every day. I couldn't be happy if I didn't see him every day. Of course sometimes it is only for a few minutes. But a few minutes with somebody one worships means a great deal."

"But you don't really worship him?"

"I do."

"How extraordinary! I thought you would never care for anything but your painting—your art, I should say. Art sounds better, doesn't it?"

"He is all my art to me now. I sometimes think, Harry, that there are only two eras of any importance in the history of the world. The first is the appearance of a new medium for art, and the second is the appearance of a new personality for art also. What the invention of oil-painting was to the Venetians, the face of Antino's was to late Greek sculpture, and the face of Dorian Gray will some day be to me. It is not merely that I paint from him, draw from him, model from him. Of course I have done all that. He has stood as Paris in dainty armour, and as Adonis with huntsman's cloak and polished boar-spear. Crowned with heavy lotus-blossoms, he has sat on the prow of Adrian's barge, looking into the green, turbid Nile. He has leaned over the still pool of some Greek woodland, and seen in the water's silent silver the wonder of his own beauty. But he is much more to me than that. I won't tell you that I am dissatisfied with what I have done of him, or that his beauty is such that art cannot express it. There is nothing that art cannot express, and I know that the work I have done since I met Dorian Gray is good work, is the best work of my life. But in some curious way—I wonder will you understand me? — his personality has suggested to me an entirely new manner in art, an entirely new mode of style. I see things differently, I think of them differently. I can now recreate life in a way that was hidden from me before. 'A dream of form in days of thought'—who is it who says that? I forget, but it is what Dorian Gray has been to me. The merely visible presence of this lad—for he seems to me little more than a lad, though he is really over twenty—his merely visible presence—ah! I wonder can you realise all that that means? Unconsciously he defines for me the lines of a fresh school, a school that is to have in itself all the passion of the romantic spirit, all the perfection of the spirit that is Greek. The harmony of soul and body— how much that is! We in our madness have separated the two, and have invented a realism that is bestial, an ideality that is void. Harry! Harry! If you only knew what Dorian Gray is to me! You remember that landscape of mine, for which Agnew offered me such a huge price, but which I would not part with? It is one of the best things I have ever done. And why is it so? Because, while I was painting it, Dorian Gray sat beside me."

"Basil, this is quite wonderful! I must see Dorian Gray."

CARSON: Now I ask you, Mr Wilde, do you consider that that description of the feeling of one man towards a youth just grown up was a proper or an improper feeling?

WILDE: I think it is the most perfect description of what an artist would feel on meeting a beautiful personality that was in some way necessary to his art and life.

CARSON: You think that is a feeling a young man should have towards another?

WILDE: Yes, as an artist.

CARSON [continuing to read from the book]:

> "Let us sit down, Dorian," said Hallward, looking pale and pained. "Let us sit down. I will sit in the shadow, and you shall sit in the sunlight. Our lives are like that. Just answer me one question. Have you noticed in the picture something that you did not like? —something that probably at first did not strike you, but that revealed itself to you suddenly?"
>
> "Basil!" cried the lad, clutching the arms of his chair with trembling hands, and gazing at him with wild, startled eyes.
>
> "I see you did. Don't speak. Wait till you hear what I have to say. It is quite true that I have worshipped you

with far more romance of feeling than a man usually gives to a friend. Somehow, I have never loved a woman. I suppose I never had time. Perhaps, as Harry says, a really 'grande passion' is the privilege of those who have nothing to do, and that is the use of the idle classes in a country. Well, from the moment I met you, your personality had the most extraordinary influence over me. I quite admit that I adored you madly, extravagantly, absurdly. I was jealous of everyone to whom you spoke. I wanted to have you all to myself. I was only happy when I was with you. When I was away from you, you were still present in my art. It was all wrong and foolish. It is all wrong and foolish still. Of course I never let you know anything about this. It would have been impossible. You would not have understood it; I did not understand it myself. One day I determined to paint a wonderful portrait of you. It was to have been my masterpiece. It is my masterpiece. But, as I worked at it, every flake and film of colour seemed to me to reveal my secret. I grew afraid that the world would know of my idolatry. I felt, Dorian, that I had told too much. Then it was that I resolved never to allow the picture to be exhibited. You were a little annoyed; but then you did not realise all that it meant to me. Harry, to whom I talked about it, laughed at me. But I did not mind that. When the picture was finished, and I sat alone with it, I felt that I was right. Well, after a few days the portrait left my studio, and as soon as I had got rid of the intolerable fascination of its presence it seemed to me that I had been foolish in imagining that I had said anything in it, more than that you were extremely good-looking and that I could paint. Even now I cannot help feeling that it is a mistake to think that the passion one feels in creation is ever really shown in the work one creates. Art is more abstract than we fancy. Form and colour tell us of form and colour—that is all. It often seems to me that art conceals the artist far more completely than it ever reveals him. And so when I got this offer from Paris I determined to make your portrait the principal thing in my exhibition. It never occurred to me that you would refuse. I see now that you were right. The picture must not be shown. You must not be angry with me, Dorian, for what I have told you. As I said to Harry once, you are made to be worshipped."

CARSON: Do you mean to say that that passage describes the natural feeling of one man towards another?

WILDE: It would be the influence produced by a beautiful personality.

CARSON: A beautiful person?

WILDE: I said a "beautiful personality". You can describe it as you like. Dorian Gray's was a most remarkable personality.

CARSON: May I take it that you, as an artist, have never known the feeling described here?

WILDE: I have never allowed any personality to dominate my art.

CARSON: Then you have never known the feeling you described?

WILDE: No. It is a work of fiction.

CARSON: So far as you are concerned you have no experience as to its being a natural feeling?

WILDE: I think it is perfectly natural for any artist to admire intensely and love a young man. It is an incident in the life of almost every artist.

CARSON: But let us go over it phrase by phrase. "I quite admit that I adored you madly." What do you say to that? Have you ever adored a young man madly?

WILDE: No, not madly; I prefer love—that is a higher form.

CARSON: Never mind about that. Let us keep down to the level we are at now?

WILDE: I have never given adoration to anybody except myself.—[Loud laughter]—

CARSON: I suppose you think that a very smart thing?

WILDE: Not at all.

CARSON: Then you have never had that feeling?

WILDE: No. The whole idea was borrowed from Shakespeare, I regret to say—yes, from Shakespeare's sonnets.

CARSON: I believe you have written an article to show that Shakespeare's sonnets were suggestive of unnatural vice?

WILDE: On the contrary; I have written an article to show that they are not. I objected to such a perversion being put upon Shakespeare.

CARSON: "I have adored you extravagantly"?—Do you mean financially?

WILDE: Oh, yes, financially!

CARSON: Do you think we are talking about finance?

WILDE: I don't know what you are talking about.

CARSON: Don't you? Well, I hope I shall make myself very plain before I have done. "I was jealous of everyone to whom you spoke." Have you ever been jealous of a young man?

WILDE: Never in my life.

CARSON: "I wanted to have you all to myself." Did you ever have that feeling?

WILDE: No; I should consider it an intense nuisance, an intense bore.

CARSON: "I grew afraid that the world would know of my idolatry." Why should he grow afraid that the world should know of it?

WILDE: Because there are people in the world who cannot understand the intense devotion, affection and admiration that an artist can feel for a wonderful and beautiful personality. These are the conditions under which we live. I regret them.

CARSON: These unfortunate people, that have not the high understanding that you have, might put it down to something wrong?

WILDE: Undoubtedly; to any point they chose. I am not concerned with the ignorance of others.

CARSON [continuing to read from *The Picture of Dorian Gray*]:

> "I think it right that you should know that the most dreadful things are being said about you in London—things that I could hardly repeat to you."
>
> "I don't wish to know anything about them. I love scandals about other people, but scandals about myself don't interest me. They have not got the charm of novelty."
>
> "They must interest you, Dorian. Every gentleman is interested in his good name. You don't want people to talk of you as something vile and degraded. Of course you have your position, and your wealth, and

all that kind of thing. But position and wealth are not everything. Mind you, I don't believe these rumours at all. At least, I can't believe them when I see you. Sin is a thing that writes itself across a man's face. It cannot be concealed. People talk of secret vices. There are no such things as secret vices. If a wretched man has a vice, it shows itself in the lines of his mouth, the droop of his eyelids, the moulding of his hands even. Somebody—I won't mention his name, but you know him—came to me last year to have his portrait done. I had never seen him before, and had never heard anything about him at the time, though I have heard a good deal since. He offered an extravagant price. I refused him. There was something in the shape of his fingers that I hated. I know now that I was quite right in what I fancied about him. His life is dreadful. But you, Dorian, with your pure, bright, innocent face, and your marvellous untroubled youth—I can't believe anything against you. And yet I see you very seldom, and you never come down to the studio now, and when I am away from you, and I hear all these hideous things that people are whispering about you, I don't know what to say. Why is it, Dorian, that a man like the Duke of Berwick leaves the room of a club when you enter it? Why is it that so many gentlemen in London will neither go to your house nor invite you to theirs? You used to be a friend of Lord Cawdor. I met him at dinner last week. Your name happened to come up in conversation, in connection with the miniatures you have lent to the exhibition at the Dudley. Cawdor curled his lip, and said that you might have the most artistic tastes, but that you were a man whom no pure-minded girl should be allowed to know, and whom no chaste woman should sit in the same room with. I reminded him that I was a friend of yours, and asked him what he meant. He told me. He told me right out before everybody. It was horrible! Why is your friendship so fateful to young men? There was that wretched boy in the Guards who committed suicide. You were his great friend. There was Sir Henry Ashton, who had to leave England with a tarnished name. You and he were inseparable. What about Adrian Singleton, and his dreadful end? What about Lord Kent's only son, and his career? I met his father yesterday in St James Street. He seemed broken with shame and sorrow. What about the young Duke of Perth? What sort of life has he got now? What gentleman would associate with him? Dorian, Dorian, your reputation is infamous."

CARSON: Does not this passage suggest a charge of unnatural vice?

WILDE: It describes Dorian Gray as a man of very corrupt influence, though there is no statement as to the nature of the influence. But as a matter of fact I do not think that one person influences another; nor do I think there is any bad influence in the world.

CARSON: A man never corrupts a youth?

WILDE: I think not.

CARSON: Nothing could corrupt him?

WILDE: If you are talking of separate ages.

CARSON: No, sir, I am talking common sense.

WILDE: I do not think one person influences another.

CARSON: You don't think that flattering a young man, making love to him, in fact, would be likely to corrupt him?

WILDE: No.

CARSON: Where was Lord Alfred Douglas staying when you wrote that letter to him?

WILDE: At the Savoy; and I was at Babbacombe, near Torquay.

CARSON: It was a letter in answer to something he had sent you?

WILDE: Yes, a poem.

CARSON: Why should a man of your age address a boy nearly 20 years younger as "My own boy"?

WILDE: I was fond of him. I have always been fond of him.

CARSON: Do you adore him?

WILDE: No, but I have always liked him. I think it is a beautiful letter. It is a poem. I was not writing an ordinary letter. You might as well cross-examine me as to whether King Lear or a sonnet of Shakespeare was proper.

CARSON: Apart from art, Mr Wilde?

WILDE: I cannot answer apart from art.

CARSON: Suppose a man who was not an artist had written this letter, would you say it was a proper letter?

WILDE: A man who was not an artist could not have written that letter.

CARSON: Why?

WILDE: Because nobody but an artist could write it. He certainly could not write the language unless he were a man of letters.

CARSON: I can suggest, for the sake of your reputation, that there is nothing very wonderful in this "red rose-leaf lips of yours"?

WILDE: A great deal depends on the way it is read.

CARSON: "Your slim gilt soul walks between passion and poetry." Is that a beautiful phrase?

WILDE: Not as you read it, Mr Carson. You read it very badly.

CARSON: I do not profess to be an artist; and when I hear you give evidence, I am glad I am not ...

SIR EDWARD CLARKE: I don't think my friend should talk like that. [To witness] Pray, do not criticise my friend's reading again.

CARSON: Is that not an exceptional letter?

WILDE: It is unique, I should say.

CARSON: Was that the ordinary way in which you carried on your correspondence?

WILDE: No; but I have often written to Lord Alfred Douglas, though I never wrote to another young man in the same way.

CARSON: Have you often written letters in the same style as this?

WILDE: I don't repeat myself in style.

CARSON: Here is another letter which I believe you also wrote to Lord Alfred Douglas. Will you read it?

WILDE: No; I decline. I don't see why I should.

CARSON: Then I will.

Savoy Hotel

Victoria Embankment, London

March 1893

Dearest of All Boys,

Your letter was delightful, red and yellow wine to
me; but I am sad and out of sorts. Bosie, you must
not make scenes with me. They kill me, they wreck
the loveliness of life. I cannot see you, so Greek and
gracious, distorted with passion. I cannot listen to
your curved lips saying hideous things to me. I would
sooner be blackmailed by every renter in London
than have you bitter, unjust, hating. . . . I must see you
soon. You are the divine thing I want, the thing of
grace and beauty; but I don't know how to do it.
Shall I come to Salisbury? My bill here is £49 for a
week. I have also got a new sitting-room over the
Thames. Why are you not here, my dear, my
wonderful boy? I fear I must leave; no money, no
credit, and a heart of lead.

Your own,

OSCAR

CARSON: Is that an ordinary letter?

WILDE: Everything I write is extraordinary. I do
not pose as being ordinary, great heavens! Ask me
any question you like about it.

CARSON: Is it the kind of letter a man writes to
another?

WILDE: It was a tender expression of my great

admiration for Lord Alfred Douglas. It was not, like the other, a prose poem.

Factual part

CARSON: Were you living at the Savoy?

WILDE: Yes, I was there for about a month, and had also my house in Tite Street. Lord Alfred had been staying with me at the Savoy immediately before I wrote that letter.

CARSON: How long had you known Wood?

WILDE: I think I met him at the end of January 1893. I met him at the Café Royal where he was sent to find me by Lord Alfred Douglas who telegraphed from Salisbury. Lord Alfred asked me to do what I could for Wood, who was seeking a post as a clerk. I do not know where he was living at that time. Taylor was living at 13 Little College Street, and I have been there to tea parties on many occasions. They were all men at the parties, but not all young men. I took Wood to supper at the Florence Restaurant in Rupert Street, because Lord Alfred had asked me to be kind to him.

CARSON: Who was Wood?

WILDE: So far as I could make out he had no occupation, but was looking for a situation. He told me he had had a clerkship. At that time he was about 23 years of age.

CARSON: Then, do I understand that the first time you met Wood you took him to supper?

WILDE: Yes, because I had been asked to be kind to him. Otherwise it was rather a bore.

CARSON: Was Taylor or anybody else there?

WILDE: No.

[In response to a series of questions from Carson, Wilde denied that he had been guilty of gross indecencies with Wood.]

CARSON: Had you a private room at the Florence?

WILDE: Yes. I went there so that I could get a cheque cashed because the next day was Sunday.

CARSON: How much did you give Wood then?

WILDE: £2.

CARSON: Why?

WILDE: Because Lord Alfred Douglas asked me to be kind to him. I don't care about different social positions.

CARSON: I suggest that you first had immoral relations with him and then gave him money?

WILDE: It is perfectly untrue.

CARSON: Did you consider that he had come to levy blackmail?

WILDE: I did; and I determined to face it.

CARSON: And the way you faced it was by giving him £15 to go to America?

WILDE: That is an inaccurate description. I saw that the letters were of no value, and I gave him the money after he had told me the pitiful tale about himself, foolishly perhaps, but out of pure kindness.

CARSON: I suggest that you gave him £30. Did you give him £5 more next day?

WILDE: Yes; he told me that after paying his passage to America he would be left almost penniless. I gave him £5.

CARSON: Had you a farewell lunch at the Florence?

WILDE: Yes.

CARSON: It was after lunch that you gave him £5?

WILDE: Yes.

CARSON: After Wood went to America, did he ask you for money?

WILDE: No.

CARSON: Did he call Taylor by his Christian name?

WILDE: Yes.

CARSON: Did Wood call you "Oscar"?

WILDE: Yes.

CARSON: What did you call Wood?

WILDE: His name is Alfred.

CARSON: Didn't you call him "Alf"?

WILDE: No, I never use abbreviations.

CARSON: Did you not think it a curious thing that a man with whom you were on such intimate terms should try to blackmail you?

WILDE: I thought it infamous, but Wood convinced me that such had not been his intention, though it was the intention of other people. Wood assured me that he had recovered all the letters.

CARSON: And then Allen came with a letter, possession of which you knew he had secured improperly?

WILDE: Yes.

CARSON: What was Allen?

WILDE: I am told he was a blackmailer.

CARSON: Was he a blackmailer?

WILDE: I never heard of him except as a blackmailer.

CARSON: Then you began to explain to the blackmailer what a loss your beautiful manuscript was?

WILDE: I described it as a beautiful work of art.

CARSON: May I ask why you gave this man, who you knew was a notorious blackmailer, ten shillings?

WILDE: I gave it out of contempt.

CARSON: Then the way you show your contempt is by paying ten shillings?

WILDE: Yes; very often.

CARSON: I suppose he was pleased with your contempt?

WILDE: Yes; he was apparently pleased at my kindness.

CARSON: Were you staying at the Albemarle Hotel about 26 February 1892?

WILDE: Yes.

CARSON: At that time were Messrs Elkin Mathews & John Lane, of Vigo Street, your publishers?

WILDE: Yes.

CARSON: Did you become fond of their office boy?

WILDE: I really do not think that that is the proper form for the question to be addressed to me in. I deny that that was the position held by Mr Edward Shelley, to whom you are referring. I object to your description.

CARSON: What age was Mr Shelley?

WILDE: I should think about 20. I first met him in October when arranging for the publication of my books. I asked him to dine with me at the Albemarle Hotel.

CARSON: Was that for the purpose of having an intellectual treat?

WILDE: Well, for him, yes. We dined in my own sitting-room, and there was one other gentleman there.

CARSON: On that occasion did you have a room leading into a bedroom?

WILDE: Yes.

CARSON: Did you give him whiskies and sodas?

WILDE: I suppose that he had whatever he wanted. I do not remember. He did not stay all night, nor did I embrace him.

CARSON: Did you ever give him money?

WILDE: Yes; on three occasions—the first time £4, the second time his railway fare to Cromer, where I invited him to meet my wife and family, and the third time £5.

CARSON: Did you think this young man of 18 was a proper or natural companion for you?

WILDE: Certainly.

CARSON: Did you give him a signed copy of the first edition of *Dorian Gray*?

WILDE: Yes.

CARSON: Did you become intimate with a young lad named Alphonse Conway at Worthing?

WILDE: Yes.

CARSON: He sold newspapers at the kiosk on the pier?

WILDE: No, I never heard that up to that time his only occupation was selling newspapers. It is the first I have heard of his connection with literature.

CARSON: What was he?

WILDE: He led a happy, idle life.

CARSON: He was a loafer, in fact? How old was he?

WILDE: He seemed to me to be just enjoying life. He was a youth of about 18.

CARSON: How did you make his acquaintance?

WILDE: When Lord Alfred Douglas and I were at Worthing, we were accustomed to go out in a boat. One day when the fishermen were launching a boat on the high beach, Conway, with another lad, assisted in getting the craft down to the water. I said to Lord Alfred Douglas: "Shall we ask them to come out for a sail?" He assented and we took them. After that Alphonse and I became great friends, and it is true that I asked him to lunch with me. He also dined at my house and lunched with me at the Marine Hotel.

CARSON: Was his conversation literary?

WILDE: On the contrary, quite simple and easily understood. He had been to school where naturally he had not learned much.

CARSON: He was a simple country lad?

WILDE: He was a nice, pleasant creature. His mother kept a lodging-house, and his desire was to go to sea. It is not true that I met him by appointment one evening and took him on the road to Lancing, kissing him and indulging in familiarities on the way.

CARSON: Did you give him anything?

WILDE: Oh, yes, but no money.

CARSON: Did you give him sums amounting to £15?

WILDE: Never. I gave him a cigarette case in which I placed a paper inscribed "Alphonse from his friend Oscar Wilde". I called him "Alphonse", but he did not call me "Oscar". I also gave him my photograph, on which I wrote "Oscar Wilde to Alphonse". I also gave him a book called *The Wreck of the Grosvenor*.

[These presents, and also a silver-mounted crook-handled grapevine stick, were produced.]

CARSON: Were you fond of this boy?

WILDE: Naturally. He had been my companion for six weeks.

CARSON: Did you take the lad to Brighton?

WILDE: Yes.

CARSON: And provided him with a suit of blue serge?

WILDE: Yes.

CARSON: And a straw hat with a band of red and blue?

WILDE: That, I think, was his unfortunate selection.

CARSON: But you paid for it?

WILDE: Yes.

CARSON: You dressed this newsboy up to take him to Brighton?

WILDE: No. I did not want him to be ashamed of his shabby clothes. He told me his father had been an electrical engineer and had died young.

CARSON: In order that he might look more like an equal?

WILDE: Oh, no! He could not look like that. No, I promised him that before I left Worthing I would take him somewhere, to some place to which he wished to go, as a reward for his being a pleasant companion to myself and my children. He chose Portsmouth, as he was anxious to go to sea, but I told him that was too far. So we went to Brighton. We dined at a restaurant and stayed the night at the Albion Hotel, where I took a sitting-room and two bedrooms. I am not sure that the bedrooms communicated by a green baize door. We returned next day. I have never taken any other boy to the Albion. I am quite certain of that.

Thursday, 4 April 1895

CARSON: You told me yesterday that you were intimate with Taylor?

WILDE: I do not call him an intimate friend. He was a friend of mine. It was he who arranged the meeting of myself with Wood about the letters at his residence, 13 Little College Street. I have known Taylor since the early part of October 1892. He used to come to my house, to my chambers, and to the Savoy. I have been several times to his house, some seven or eight times, perhaps.

CARSON: You used to go to tea parties there— afternoon tea parties?

WILDE: Yes.

CARSON: How many rooms did he occupy?

WILDE: He had the upper part of the house—two stories. He had a bedroom, a sitting-room, a bathroom and a kitchen. I think he did not keep a servant.

CARSON: Did he use to do his own cooking?

WILDE: I don't know. I don't think he did anything wrong.

CARSON: I have not suggested that he did.

WILDE: Well, cooking is an art.

CARSON: Another art? Did he always open the door to you?

WILDE: No; sometimes he did; sometimes his friends did.

CARSON: Did his rooms strike you as being peculiar?

WILDE: No, except that he displayed more taste than usual.

CARSON: There was rather elaborate furniture in the room, was there not?

WILDE: The rooms were furnished in good taste.

CARSON: Is it true that he never admitted daylight into them?

WILDE: Really, I don't know what you mean.

CARSON: Well, was there always candle or gas light there?

WILDE: No.

CARSON: Did you ever see the rooms lighted otherwise than by gas or candles whether by day or night?

WILDE: Yes, certainly.

CARSON: Did you ever see the curtains drawn back in the sitting-room?

WILDE: When I went to see Taylor, it was generally in the winter about 5 p.m.— tea-time—but I am under the impression of having seen him earlier in the day when it was daylight.

CARSON: Are you prepared to say that you ever saw the curtains otherwise than drawn across?

WILDE: Yes, I think so.

CARSON: It would not be true, then, to say that he always had a double lot of curtains drawn across the windows, and the room, day or night, artificially lighted?

WILDE: I don't think so.

CARSON: Can you declare specifically that any daylight was ever admitted into the room?

WILDE: Well, I can't say as to that.

CARSON: Who was there when you went in the daylight?

WILDE: I think Mr Taylor only.

CARSON: Can you recall any specific time at which you saw daylight enter that room?

WILDE: Yes; it was a Monday in March. Nobody else was there. In the winter the curtains would naturally be drawn.

CARSON: Were the rooms strongly perfumed?

WILDE: Yes, I have known him to burn perfumes. I would not say the rooms were always perfumed. I am in the habit of burning perfumes in my own rooms.

CARSON: Did you ever meet Wood there?

WILDE: I saw Wood there only on one occasion when I met him at tea.

CARSON: Did you ever meet a man named Sidney Mavor there?

WILDE: Yes.

CARSON: How old was he?

WILDE: About 25 or 26.

CARSON: Is he your friend still?

WILDE: Yes.

CARSON: Did you know that Taylor had a lady's costume—a lady's fancy dress—in his rooms?

WILDE: No.

CARSON: Did you ever see him with one on?

WILDE: No. I was never told that he had such dresses. He is a man of great taste and intelligence, and I know he was brought up at a good English school.

CARSON: Is he a literary man?

WILDE: I have never seen any created work of his.

CARSON: Did you discuss literature with him?

WILDE: He used to listen. He was a very artistic, pleasant fellow.

CARSON: Was he an artist?

WILDE: Not in the sense of creating anything. He was extremely intellectual and clever, and I liked him very much.

CARSON: Did you get him to arrange dinners at which you could meet young men?

WILDE: No.

CARSON: But you have dined with young men?

WILDE: Often. Ten or a dozen times, perhaps, at Kettner's, the Solferino, and the Florence.

CARSON: Always in a private room?

WILDE: Generally, not always; but I prefer a private room.

CARSON: Did you send this telegram to Taylor: "Obliged to see Tree at five o'clock, so don't come to Savoy. Let me know at once about Fred. Oscar"?

WILDE: I do not recollect it.

CARSON: Who was Fred?

WILDE: A young man to whom I was introduced by the gentleman whose name was written down yesterday. His other name was Atkins.

CARSON: Were you very familiar with him?

WILDE: I liked him. I never had any trouble about him.

CARSON: Now, did you know that Taylor was being watched by the police?

WILDE: No, I never heard that.

CARSON: Did you know that Taylor and Parker were arrested in a raid upon a house in Fitzroy Square last year?

WILDE: Yes.

CARSON: Now, did you not know that Taylor was notorious for introducing young men to older men?

WILDE: I never heard that in my life. He has introduced young men to me.

CARSON: How many has he introduced to you?

WILDE: Do you mean of those mentioned in this case?

CARSON: No; young men with whom you afterwards became intimate?

WILDE: About five.

CARSON: Were these young men all about 20?

WILDE: Yes; 20 or 22. I like the society of young men.

CARSON: Among these five did Taylor introduce you to Charles Parker?

WILDE: Yes.

CARSON: Did you become friendly with him?

WILDE: Yes, he was one with whom I became friendly.

CARSON: Did you know that Parker was a gentleman's servant out of employment?

WILDE: No.

CARSON: But if he were, you would still have become friendly with him?

WILDE: Yes. I would become friendly with any human being I liked.

CARSON: How old was he?

WILDE: Really, I do not keep a census.

CARSON: Never mind about a census. Tell me how old he was?

WILDE: I should say he was about 20. He was young, and that was one of his attractions.

CARSON: Was he intellectual? Was he an educated man?

WILDE: Culture was not his strong point. He was not an artist. Education depends on what one's standard is.

CARSON: Did you become friendly with Parker's brother?

WILDE: Yes. They were my guests, and as such I became friendly with them.

CARSON: On the very first occasion that you saw them?

WILDE: Yes. It was Taylor's birthday, and I asked him to dinner, telling him to bring any of his friends.

CARSON: Did you know that one Parker was a gentleman's valet, and the other a groom?

WILDE: I did not know it, but if I had I should not have cared. I didn't care twopence what they were. I liked them. I have a passion to civilise the community.

CARSON: What enjoyment was it to you to entertain grooms and coachmen?

WILDE: The pleasure to me was being with those who are young, bright, happy, careless, and free. I do not like the sensible and I do not like the old.

CARSON: You did the honours to the valet and the groom?

WILDE: I entertained Taylor and his two guests.

CARSON: In a private room, of course?

WILDE: Yes, certainly.

CARSON: Did you give them an intellectual treat?

WILDE: They seemed deeply impressed.

CARSON: During the dinner did you become more intimate with Charles than the other?

WILDE: I liked him better.

CARSON: Did Charles Parker call you "Oscar"?

WILDE: Yes. I like to be called "Oscar" or "Mr Wilde".

CARSON: You had wine?

WILDE: Of course.

CARSON: Was there plenty of champagne?

WILDE: Well, I did not press wine upon them.

CARSON: You did not stint them?

WILDE: What gentleman would stint his guests?

CARSON: Now, after dinner, did you say, referring to Charles Parker, in the presence of Taylor and William Parker, the brother, "This is the boy for me"?

WILDE: Certainly not.

CARSON: And did you ask Charles, "Will you come with me"?

WILDE: No. After dinner I went back to the Savoy Hotel, but I did not take Charles Parker with me.

CARSON: Did you not drive him to the Savoy?

WILDE: No; he did not come to the Savoy at all.

CARSON: Did any of these men who visited you at the Savoy have whiskies and sodas and iced champagne?

WILDE: I can't say what they had.

CARSON: Do you drink champagne yourself?

WILDE: Yes; iced champagne is a favourite drink of mine—strongly against my doctor's orders.

CARSON: Never mind your doctor's orders, sir?

WILDE: I never do.

CARSON: Did improprieties take place there?

WILDE: None whatever.

CARSON: What was there in common between this young man and yourself? What attraction had he for you?

WILDE: I delight in the society of people much younger than myself. I like those who may be called idle and careless. I recognise no social distinctions at all of any kind; and to me youth, the mere fact of youth, is so wonderful that I would sooner talk to a young man for half-an-hour than be—well, cross-examined in Court.

CARSON: Do I understand that even a young boy you might pick up in the street would be a pleasing companion?

WILDE: I would talk to a street arab, with pleasure.

CARSON: You would talk to a street arab?

WILDE: If he would talk to me. Yes, with pleasure.

CARSON: And take him into your rooms?

WILDE: Be it so.

CARSON: When did you see Charles Parker last?

WILDE: I don't think I have seen him since February of last year.

CARSON: Did you ever hear what became of him?

WILDE: I heard that he had gone into the army—enlisted as a private.

CARSON: You saw in the papers of the arrest of Taylor and Parker?

WILDE: Yes; I read that they were arrested.

CARSON: You know that they were charged with felonious practices?

WILDE: I knew nothing of the charges.

CARSON: That when they were arrested they were in company with several men in women's clothing?

WILDE: I read of it in the newspapers that two men, in women's clothes, music-hall artistes, drove up to the house and were arrested outside.

CARSON: Did you not think it a somewhat serious thing that Mr Taylor, your great friend, and Charles Parker, another great friend, should have been arrested in a police raid?

WILDE: I was very much distressed at the time and wrote to him, but the magistrates took a different view of the case, because they dismissed the charge. It made no difference to my friendship for him.

CARSON: When did you first meet Fred Atkins?

WILDE: In October 1892. He told me he was connected with a firm of bookmakers. He was about

19 or 20. I was introduced to him in the rooms of a gentleman in Margaret Street, off Regent Street. I did not know him through making bets. I did not ask him to dinner on the first day I met him. I met him at a dinner given by another gentleman whose rooms I met him in first. I was friendly with Atkins on that occasion. I called him "Fred" and he called me "Oscar". He was in employment, but apologised and said he neglected his business.

CARSON: Did he seem to you an idle fellow?

WILDE: Well, yes. But he was ambitious to go on the music-hall stage. We did not discuss literature. I would not have allowed him to. The art of the music-hall was as far as he got.

CARSON: Did you ask him to go to Paris with you?

WILDE: I must explain. One Sunday I saw him and the gentleman, who has been mentioned, lunching at the Café Royal. I was going to Paris on my own account in reference to the publication of a book. This other gentleman was also going to Paris about a position on Dalziel's Agency. It was suggested that we should all go together, as he had promised to take Atkins. It was arranged that we should go on a Monday, but subsequently the gentleman found that he could not go until Tuesday or Wednesday. Then, as Atkins seemed very much disappointed, the gentleman asked me if I would take Fred over. I said, "With the greatest pleasure", and I took him.

CARSON: How long had you known Atkins then?

WILDE: About a fortnight. We went by the Club train. I paid for his ticket, but the money was refunded to me afterwards by the gentleman. I did not suggest to Atkins that he should go as my secretary—ridiculous, it's childish to ask such a thing. I took him to the same rooms I occupied in the hotel—29 boulevard des Capucines. I engaged three bedrooms, having one in reserve. They all three opened on to each other. I never asked Fred to copy some manuscript for me. I took him to lunch at the Café Julien. He was practically my guest, as representing the gentleman I have mentioned.

CARSON: After lunch did you suggest that Atkins should have his hair curled?

WILDE: He suggested it himself, and I said it would be very unbecoming, and I told him it was a silly thing to do, an absurd thing. I should have been very angry if he had had his hair curled.

CARSON: You dined with him?

WILDE: Yes.

CARSON: Gave him an excellent dinner?

WILDE: I never had anything else. I do everything excellently.

CARSON: Did you give him plenty of wine at dinner?

WILDE: As I have said before, any one who dines at my table is not stinted in wine. If you mean, did I ply him with wine, I say "No!" It's monstrous, and I won't have it.

CARSON: I have not suggested it.

WILDE: But you have suggested it before.

CARSON: Did you ask him to promise that he would say nothing about going to Paris?

WILDE: No. I thought it was the great event of his life, as it was.

CARSON: Did you consider Atkins respectable?

WILDE: Respectable? Yes. I thought him pleasant and young. He was good-natured, and was going on to the music-hall stage. I heard him sing. He was interesting.

CARSON: Was he alone when he came to you at St James's Place?

WILDE: No; I think he was accompanied by the young actor. I will swear that Atkins was not alone in the room with me.

CARSON: Did any improprieties ever take place between you and Atkins?

WILDE: None whatever.

CARSON: Do you know Walter Grainger?

WILDE: Yes.

CARSON: How old is he?

WILDE: He was about 16 when I knew him. He was a servant at a certain house in High Street, Oxford, where Lord Alfred Douglas had rooms. I have stayed there several times. Grainger waited at table. I never dined with him. If it is one's duty to serve, it is one's duty to serve; and if it is one's pleasure to dine, it is one's pleasure to dine.

CARSON: Did you ever kiss him?

WILDE: Oh, dear no. He was a peculiarly plain boy. He was, unfortunately, extremely ugly. I pitied him for it.

CARSON: Was that the reason why you did not kiss him?

WILDE: Oh, Mr Carson, you are pertinently insolent.

CARSON: Did you say that in support of your statement that you never kissed him?

WILDE: No. It is a childish question.

CARSON: Did you ever put that forward as a reason why you never kissed the boy?

WILDE: Not at all.

CARSON: Why, sir, did you mention that this boy was extremely ugly?

WILDE: For this reason. If I were asked why I did not kiss a doormat, I should say because I do not like to kiss doormats. I do not know why I mentioned that he was ugly, except that I was stung by the insolent question you put to me and the way you have insulted me throughout this hearing. Am I to be cross-examined because I do not like it?

CARSON: Why did you mention his ugliness?

WILDE: It is ridiculous to imagine that any such thing could have occurred under any circumstances.

CARSON: Then why did you mention his ugliness, I ask you?

WILDE: Perhaps you insulted me by an insulting question.

CARSON: Was that a reason why you should say the boy was ugly?

[The witness began several answers almost inarticulately, and finished none of them. Carson repeated sharply: "Why? Why? Why did you add that?" At last the witness answered.]

WILDE: You sting me and insult me and try to unnerve me; and at times one says things flippantly when one ought to speak more seriously. I admit it.

CARSON: Then you said it flippantly?

WILDE: Oh, yes, it was a flippant answer. No indecencies ever took place between myself and Grainger. I went down in June 1893 to stay at a cottage at Goring. I brought over Grainger as under-butler. He had asked me to get him a situation. I never on any occasion asked him to come into my bedroom. I don't know where the butler I had then is now.

CARSON: Did you know a masseur at the Savoy named Antonio Migge?

WILDE: Yes. He used occasionally to massage me in the morning. I stayed at the Savoy in March 1893 but never on that occasion brought boys into my bedroom there.

CARSON: Did you ever bring boys into your rooms at the hotel in Paris?

WILDE: Never.

CARSON: Or into your sitting-room?

WILDE: What do you mean by boys?

CARSON: Boys of 18 or 20?

WILDE: Oh, yes; many called to see me.

CARSON: Did any of them come late at night—twelve or one o'clock—and stay till four in the morning?

WILDE: Certainly not.

CARSON: Is it not true that there has been a scandal at the Savoy Hotel?

WILDE: None whatever.

OPENING SPEECH FOR THE DEFENCE

MR EDWARD CARSON: May it please you, my lord, gentlemen of the jury. In appearing in this case for Lord Queensberry I cannot but feel that a very grave responsibility rests upon me. So far as Lord Queensberry is concerned, in any act he has done, in any letter he has written, or in the matter of the card which has put him in the present position, he withdraws nothing. He has done all those things with a premeditation and a determination, at all risks and at all hazards, to try to save his son. Whether Lord Queensberry was right or whether he was wrong, you have probably to some extent information on which you can found a judgement. I must say for Lord Queensberry, notwithstanding many elements of prejudice which my learned friend, Sir Edward Clarke, thought fit to introduce into the case in his opening speech, that Lord Queensberry's conduct in this respect has been absolutely consistent all through, and if the facts which he stated in his letters as to Mr Wilde's reputation and acts are correct, then not only was he justified in doing what he could to cut short what would probably prove a most disastrous acquaintance for his son, but in taking every step which suggested itself to him to bring about an inquiry into the acts and doings of Mr Wilde.

Gentlemen, from beginning to end Lord Queensberry, in dealing with Mr Oscar Wilde, has been influenced by one hope alone—that of saving his son. What is Mr Wilde's own case? The prosecutor has said that up to a certain date he was on terms of friendship with Lord Queensberry, and therefore there were no circumstances rendering his lordship liable to the accusation that what he had done in the present case was done from malice arising out of disagreement. Lord Queensberry came to know of Mr Wilde's character, of the scandals in connection with the Savoy Hotel, that the prosecutor had been going about with young men who were not co-equal with him in position or in age, and that he had been associating with men who, it will be proved beyond doubt, are some of the most immoral characters in London. I refer above all to the man Taylor, a most notorious character—as the police will tell the Court—who occupied rooms which were nothing more or less than a shameful den. Whether Taylor was or was not a procurer in this sense, the fact remains that on Tuesday last—2 April—he was in company with Mr Wilde at the latter's house in Tite Street and that he has not been produced by the prosecution. Taylor has in fact been the right-hand man of Mr Wilde in all the orgies in which artists and valets have taken part; and, if opportunity had only been given of cross-examining him, it might have been possible to get from him at least something as to what was going on at Fitzroy Square on the night of the raid there last year.

Taylor is really the pivot of the case for the simple reason that when the various witnesses for the defence are called and examined—as unfortunately will be necessary—as to the practices of Mr Oscar Wilde, it will be found that it was Taylor who introduced the young men to the prosecutor. Mr Oscar Wilde has undertaken to prove enough to send Lord Queensberry to gaol and to brand him as a criminal, but it is remarkable that the only witness who could have supported Mr Wilde's asseverance of innocence has not been called. Yet Taylor is still a friend of Mr Wilde, and nothing, said the prosecutor, has happened to interrupt their friendship.

It will be painful to be compelled to ask the various witnesses that will be called to describe the manner in which Mr Wilde has acted towards them; but, before the case is ended, you will be obliged to hear a good deal more of the extraordinary den which Taylor kept in Little College Street. Therefore, it is above all things necessary, when we have so much proved by his own admissions, that Mr Wilde should bring any witness he can to bear out his own explanations. We have heard a great deal of the gentleman whose name was written down. On each occasion when it was convenient to introduce somebody, this was the name which Mr Wilde gave because he was out of the country. But Taylor is still in the country. Why has he not been called?

Let us contrast the position which Mr Wilde took up in cross-examination as to his books, which are for the select and not for the ordinary individual, with the position he assumed as to the young men to whom he was introduced and those he picked up for himself. His books were written by an artist for artists; his words were not for Philistines or illiterates. Contrast that with the way in which Mr Wilde chose his companions! He took up with Charles Parker, a gentleman's servant, whose brother was a gentleman's servant; with young Alphonse Conway, who sold papers on the pier at Worthing; and with Scarfe, also a gentleman's servant.

Then his excuse was no longer that he was dwelling in regions of art but that he had such a noble, such a democratic soul—[Laughter]—that he drew no social distinctions, and that it was quite as much pleasure to have the sweeping boy from the streets to lunch or dine with him as the greatest *littérateur* or artist.

In my judgement, if the case had rested on Mr Wilde's literature alone, Lord Queensberry would have been absolutely justified in the course he has taken. Lord Queensberry has undertaken to prove that Mr Wilde has been "posing" as guilty of certain vices. Mr Wilde never complained of the immorality of the story "The Priest and the Acolyte", which appeared in *The Chameleon*. He knows no distinction, in fact, between a moral and an immoral book. Nor does he care whether the article is in its very terms blasphemous. All that Mr Wilde says is that he did not approve of the story from a literary point of view. What is that story? It is a story of the love of a priest for the acolyte who attended him at Mass. Exactly the same idea that runs through the two letters to Lord Alfred Douglas runs through that story and also through *The Picture of Dorian Gray*. When the boy was discovered in the priest's bed, the priest made exactly the same defence as Mr Wilde has made—that the world does not understand the beauty of this love. The same idea runs through these two letters which Mr Wilde has called beautiful, but which I call an abominable piece of disgusting immorality.

Moreover, there is in this same *Chameleon* a poem which shows some justification for the frightful anticipations which Lord Queensberry entertained for his son. The poem was written by Lord Alfred Douglas and was seen by Mr Wilde before its publication. Is it not a terrible thing that a young man on the threshold of life, who has for several years been dominated by Oscar Wilde and has been "adored and loved" by Oscar Wilde, as the two letters prove, should thus show the tendency of his mind upon this frightful subject? What would be the horror of any man whose son wrote such a poem?

Passing now to *The Picture of Dorian Gray*, it is the tale of a beautiful young man who, by the conversation of one who has great literary power and ability to speak in epigrams—just as Mr Wilde has—and who, by reading of exactly the same kind as that in "Phrases and Philosophies for the Use of the Young", has his eyes opened to what they are pleased to call the "delights of the world". If *Dorian Gray* is a book which it can be conclusively proved advocates the vice imputed to Mr Wilde, what answer, then, is there to Lord Queensberry's plea of justification?

The turning of one of Wilde's letters to Lord Alfred Douglas into a sonnet was a very thinly veiled attempt to get rid of the character of that letter. A more thinly veiled attempt to cover its real nature has never been made in a Court of Justice. I have some difficulty in understanding why my learned friend Sir Edward Clarke has referred to that letter at all. Perhaps he thought the defence had the letter, and that it would be better to give an explanation of it; but if that is so, it is futile because, for the letter which the defence did produce, my learned friend has no explanation.

My learned friend has referred to "a man named Wood" as being supposed to have taken out of the pocket of Lord Alfred Douglas correspondence which had passed between him and Wilde. But who is Wood? Why, he too is "Fred", one of Wilde's bosom companions, a friend of Taylor, one of the Little College Street lot! What, then, was the case of the strained relations between Wilde and Wood? Why did Wilde give Wood £15? When I state that, previous to the possession of those letters, Wood had been carrying on certain practices with Wilde, you will have the key to the whole situation. That is one reason why Wilde would be anxious to get the letters at any cost, and when Wood came to levy blackmail, then Mr Wilde became very anxious that the man should leave the country. So he paid his passage and, after a farewell luncheon, he shipped him off to New York and, I suppose, hoped that he would never see him again.—[Counsel paused a moment.]—But, gentlemen, as a matter of fact, Wood is here and will be examined before you.—[Noise and excitement in the courtroom]—I am not here to say anything has ever happened between Lord Alfred Douglas and Mr Oscar Wilde. God forbid! But everything shows that the young man was in a dangerous position in that he acquiesced in the domination of Mr Wilde, a man of great ability and attainments. Against that letter written by Mr Wilde to Lord Queensberry's son, Lord Queensberry protested; and I wish to know, gentlemen, are you, for that protest, going to send Lord Queensberry to gaol? Lord Queensberry was determined to bring the matter to an issue, and what other way was open to him than that which he had chosen?

Before you condemn Lord Queensberry I ask you to read Wilde's letter and to say whether the gorge of any father ought not to rise. I ask you to bear in mind that Lord Queensberry's son was so dominated by Wilde that he threatened to shoot his own father. Gentlemen, Lord Queensberry did what he has done most deliberately, and he is not afraid to abide by the issue which he has raised in this Court. When you have heard Wood's evidence, the whole story of the payment of those sums of money by Wilde, and the mystery of those letters, will be explained; and the suggestion that they were valuable manuscripts, which Wilde desired to obtain, will be dissipated. As a matter of fact, Wilde knew that we had all the evidence, and he preferred to discount it as far as possible in advance.

Friday, 5 April 1895

CARSON: May it please your lordship, gentlemen of the jury. Yesterday, when it came to the usual time for the adjournment of the Court, I had dealt as fully as I intended to deal with the question of Mr Wilde's connection with the literature and the two letters which have been produced in this case and I had almost hoped that I had sufficiently demonstrated to you upon that matter that so far as Lord Queensberry was concerned, he was absolutely justified in bringing to a climax in the way he did this question of the connection between Mr Oscar Wilde and his son. I have unfortunately a more painful part of the case now to approach. It will be my painful duty to bring before you young men, one after another, who have been in the hands of Mr Wilde, to tell their unhappy tales. It is, even for an advocate, a very distasteful task. But let those who are inclined to condemn these young men for being dominated, misled, and corrupted by Mr Wilde, remember the relative position of the two parties. Let them say whether those young men were not more sinned against than sinning. I am not going in any great detail now to criticise the evidence of Mr Oscar Wilde in relation to the several transactions on which he was cross-examined. But there are some general observations applicable to all the cases that have been raised against Mr Wilde. There is in point of fact a startling similarity between each of them on his own admission which must lead you, gentlemen, to draw the most painful conclusions. There is the fact that in no one of these cases were these parties on an equality in any way with Mr Wilde; they are none of them educated parties with whom he would naturally associate, and they are not his equal in years. But on the other hand, gentlemen, you will have observed a curious similarity in the ages of each of them.

Mr Wilde has said that there is something beautiful, something charming about youth which led him to adopt the course he did. But was Mr

Wilde unable to find more suitable companions, at the same time young and charming, in the ranks of his own class? Why, the thing is absurd. His excuse in the witness-box is only a travesty of the facts.

Who are all these young men—these lads? There is Wood. Of his history Mr Wilde has told us that he knows nothing. So far as Mr Wilde knew, Wood was a clerk out of employment. Who is Parker? Mr Wilde professed the same ignorance as to that youth. Who is Scarfe? Exactly in the same way Mr Wilde knew nothing of him. He only knew that he was out of employment. Alphonse Conway he picked up by chance on the beach at Worthing. All the young men introduced to Mr Wilde were of something like 18 or 20 years of age. The manner of their introduction, and the way in which they were subsequently treated with money and presents, all lead up to the conclusion that there was something unnatural in the relations between Mr Wilde and these young men. Take the case of Parker. How did Mr Wilde get to know that young man? Parker was a gentleman's servant out of employment; and what idea could Taylor have had of Mr Wilde's tastes when, on being invited by Wilde to ask his friends to a birthday dinner, he introduced as his guests a groom and a valet? If it were true, as undoubtedly it was, that Taylor first met the two young men in a restaurant in Piccadilly, why did he—if he knew that Mr Wilde was an artistic and literary man, and, what was more, an upright man—bring the couple to dine with Mr Wilde? There can be no explanation of the facts but this: that Taylor was a procurer for Wilde, as he undoubtedly was.

Parker will be called to tell his unfortunate story—his story that he was poor, out of place and that he fell a victim to Mr Wilde. Upon the first occasion that Mr Wilde met Parker, the valet, he addressed him as "Charlie", and Charlie addressed Mr Wilde, the distinguished dramatist, whose name at the time was being mentioned in the highest circles in London for his plays and his literary work, as "Oscar".

I do not wish to say anything about Mr Wilde's theories as to putting an end to social distinctions. A man of noble and generous instincts might be able to break down all social barriers; but there is one thing plain in this case, and that is that Mr Wilde's conduct to the young men introduced to him was not instigated by any generous instincts. If Mr Wilde wanted to assist Parker, if he were interested in him, if he wanted to find him employment, was it doing the lad a good turn to take him to a restaurant and prime him with champagne and a good dinner? Was that the work of charity and sympathy one would expect a man in Mr Wilde's position to extend to another man like Parker? All the ridiculous explanation of Mr Wilde will not bear one moment's explanation as to what he was doing in his suite of rooms at the Savoy. The Savoy is a large place, with plenty of room to move about in, and there is no doubt that, without leading people to suspect anything, Mr Wilde could have brought young men into his rooms.

Parker will tell you that when he went to the Savoy with Mr Wilde he had whiskies and sodas and iced champagne—that iced champagne in which Mr Wilde indulged contrary to his doctor's orders. Parker will furthermore tell you of the shocking acts he was led by Mr Wilde to perpetrate on that occasion. Mr Wilde was asked in cross-examination: "Is it not true that there has been a scandal at the Savoy Hotel?" "None whatever," said Mr Wilde. But about that very extraordinary thing Lord Queensberry has referred in his letter dated 6 July 1894. It might have been that no one had seen Mr Wilde turned out into the street, but such kind of gossip could not have arisen without going abroad and being reported in the circles in which Lord Queensberry mixed. The wonder is not that the gossip reached Lord Queensberry, but that, after it was known, this man Wilde should have been tolerated in society in London for the length of time he has. Well, I shall prove that Mr Wilde brought boys into the Savoy Hotel. The masseur of that establishment—a most respectable man—and other servants will be called to prove the character of Mr Wilde's relations with his visitors. Is there any wonder that reports of a scandal at the Savoy should have reached Lord Queensberry, whose son was living a portion of the time at the hotel?

Mr Wilde has not ventured to deny that Parker has dined with him, has been in his company, and has lunched with him at his rooms and at the Savoy. Mr Wilde, seeing the importance of these facts, has made a clean breast of it. "Oh, yes," he said, "they were perfectly innocent, nay, more, they were generous actions on my part." It is remarkable that Mr Wilde has given no account as to what he was doing in those rooms at the Savoy. Parker will tell you what happened on arriving there. He has since enlisted in the army and bears a good character. Mr Wilde himself said that Parker is a respectable man. Parker will reluctantly present himself to tell you his story.

As to the boy Conway, Conway was not procured by Taylor—he was procured by Mr Wilde himself. Has there ever been confessed in a Court of Justice a more audacious story than that confessed to by Mr Wilde in relation to Conway? He met the boy, he said, on the beach at Worthing. He knew nothing whatsoever about him, excepting that he assisted in launching the boats. Conway's real history is that he sold newspapers at Worthing at the kiosk on the pier. What a flippant answer it was that Mr Wilde gave to the question, "Did you know that Conway sold newspapers?" when he replied: "I did not know that he had previous connection with literature." Perhaps, in that, Mr Wilde thought he was clever at repartee, and was scoring off counsel whose duty it was to cross-examine him. But here are the facts. After helping Mr Wilde to get out his boat, an intimacy sprang up between them, and within a day or two Conway was taken by Mr Wilde to the house he was occupying. If the evidence of Mr Wilde was true—and I sincerely hope it is not—Conway was introduced to Mrs Wilde and her two sons, aged nine and ten. Now, it is clear that Mr Wilde could not take about the boy Conway in the condition he found him in. So what did he do? And it is here that the disgraceful audacity of the man comes in. Mr Wilde procured the boy a suit of clothes to dress him up like a gentleman's son, put some public school colours upon his hat and generally made him look like a lad fit and proper to associate with Mr Oscar Wilde. The whole thing in its audacity is almost past belief. Why, if the defence had proved the fact, instead of getting it from the mouth of the prosecutor, you would have said it was almost incredible. But why did Mr Wilde dress up Conway? If Mr Wilde were really anxious to assist Conway, the very worst thing he could have done was to take the lad out of his proper sphere, to begin by giving him champagne luncheons, taking him to his hotel and treating him in a manner in which the boy could never in the future expect to live.

WITHDRAWAL OF PROSECUTION

SIR EDWARD CLARKE: May I claim your lordship's indulgence while I interpose to make a statement, which, of course, is made under a feeling of very great responsibility?

My learned friend Mr Carson yesterday addressed the jury upon the question of the literature involved in this case, and upon the inferences to be drawn from the admissions made with regard to letters written by Mr Oscar Wilde; and my friend began his address this morning by saying that he hoped that yesterday he had said enough in dealing with those topics to induce the jury to relieve him from the necessity of dealing in detail with the other issues in this case. I think it must have been present to your lordship's mind that those who represent Mr Wilde in this case have before them a very terrible anxiety. They cannot conceal from themselves that the judgement that might be formed on that literature, and upon the conduct which has been admitted, might not improbably induce the jury to say that Lord Queensberry in using the word "posing" was using a word for which there was sufficient justification to entitle the father, who used those words under these circumstances, to the utmost consideration and to be relieved of a criminal charge in respect of his statement. And with this in our clear view, I and my learned friends associated with me in this matter had to look forward to this—that a verdict given in favour of defendant upon that part of the case might be interpreted outside as a conclusive finding with regard to all parts of the case.

And the position in which we stood was this— that, without expecting a verdict in this case, we should be going through, day after day, an investigation of matters of the most appalling character.

Under these circumstances I hope your lordship will think I am taking the right course, which I take after communicating with Mr Oscar Wilde.

That is to say that, having regard to what has been referred to by my learned friend in respect of the matters connected with the literature and the letters, I feel we could not resist a verdict of not guilty in this case—not guilty having reference to the word "posing". Under these circumstances I hope you will think I am not going beyond the bounds of my duty, and that I am doing something to save, to prevent, what would be a most horrible task, however it might close, if I now interpose and say on behalf of Mr Oscar Wilde that I would ask to withdraw from the prosecution. And if you do not think that at this time of the case, and after what has taken place—if you do not think I ought to be allowed to do that on his behalf, I am prepared to submit to a verdict of not guilty, having reference, if to any part of the particulars at all, to that part of the particulars connected with the publication of *The Picture of Dorian Gray* and the publication of *The Chameleon*. I trust that this may make an end of the case.

MR EDWARD CARSON: I do not know that I have any right whatever to interfere in any way with this application my learned friend has made. I can only say, as far as Lord Queensberry is concerned, that if there is a plea of not guilty, a plea which involves that he has succeeded in his plea of justification, I am quite satisfied. Of course, my learned friend will admit that we must succeed upon the plea in the manner in which he has stated; and that being so, it rests entirely with your lordship as to whether the course suggested by my learned friend is to be taken.

MR JUSTICE COLLINS: In as much as the prosecutor in this case is prepared to acquiesce in a verdict of not guilty against the accused, I do not think it is any part of the function of the judge or of the jury to insist on going through prurient details which can have no bearing upon a matter already concluded by the assent of the prosecutor to an adverse verdict. But as to the jury putting any limitation upon the verdict of justification of the charge, which is "posing as a sodomite"—if that is justified, it is justified; if it is not, it is not. And the verdict of the jury must be "Guilty" or "Not Guilty". There can be no terms and no limitations. The verdict must be "Guilty" or "Not Guilty". I understand him to assent to a verdict of Not Guilty, and of course the jury will return that.

CLARKE: The verdict is "Not Guilty".

MR JUSTICE COLLINS: The verdict is "Not Guilty", but it is arrived at by that process. I shall have to tell the jury that justification was proved; and that it was true in substance and in fact that the prosecutor had "posed" as a sodomite. I shall also have to tell them that they will have to find that the statement was published in such a manner as to be for the public benefit. If they find on these two points, the verdict will be "Not Guilty".

[To the jury] Your verdict will be "Not Guilty"; but there are other matters which have to be determined with reference to the specific finding of complete justification, and, as I told you, that involves that the statement is true in fact and substance, and that the publication is for the public benefit. These are the facts on which you will have to find, and if you find them in favour of the defendant, your verdict will be "Not Guilty". You will have to say whether you find complete justification has been proved.

[The jury consulted together briefly.]

CLERK OF ARRAIGNS: Gentlemen of the Jury, do you find the plea of justification has been proved or not?

FOREMAN OF THE JURY: Yes.

CLERK OF ARRAIGNS: And do you find defendant not guilty?

FOREMAN: Yes.—[Applause]—

CLERK OF ARRAIGNS: And that is the verdict of you all?

FOREMAN: Yes.

CLERK OF ARRAIGNS: And also that it was published for the public benefit?

FOREMAN: Yes.

CARSON: Of course, the costs of the defence will follow.

MR JUSTICE COLLINS: Yes.

MR CHARLES GILL: And Lord Queensberry may be discharged.

MR JUSTICE COLLINS: Oh, certainly.

The Court adjourned.

Edward Carson had forwarded to the Director of Public Prosecutions copies of the statements of the witnesses the defence had planned to produce. On 6 April 1895 Wilde was arrested and charged with offences under Section 11 of the Criminal Law Amendment Act 1885. No bail was granted and he was detained on remand at Holloway.

PART III

❧

THE CRIMINAL TRIALS OF OSCAR WILDE

TRANSCRIPT EXCERPTS FROM
THE FIRST CRIMINAL TRIAL

The first criminal trial of Oscar Wilde was held at the Old Bailey, 26 April–1 May 1895. Wilde and Alfred Taylor, the procurer of young men for Wilde, faced 25 counts of gross indecencies and conspiracy to commit gross indecencies. Sir Edward Clarke again acted as attorney for Wilde. The prosecution was led by Charles Gill.

TESTIMONY OF PROSECUTION
WITNESS CHARLES PARKER

Examination by Mr Charles Gill

PARKER: I am 21 years of age. I have a brother, William. I have been engaged as a valet and my brother as a groom. At the beginning of 1893 I was out of employment. I remember one day at that time being with my brother at the St James's Restaurant, in the bar. While there Taylor came up and spoke to us. He was an entire stranger. He passed the compliments of the day, and asked us to have a drink. We got into conversation with him. He spoke about men.

GILL: In what way?

PARKER: He called attention to the prostitutes who frequent Piccadilly Circus and remarked: "I can't understand sensible men wasting their money on painted trash like that. Many do though. But there are a few who know better. Now, you could get money in a certain way easily enough if you cared to." I understood to what Taylor alluded and made a coarse reply.

GILL: I am obliged to ask you what it was you actually said?

PARKER: I do not like to say.

GILL: You were less squeamish at the time, I dare say. I ask you for the words?

PARKER: I said that if any old gentleman with money took a fancy to me, I was agreeable. I was agreeable. I was terribly hard up.

GILL: What did Taylor say?

PARKER: He laughed and said that men far cleverer, richer and better than I preferred things of that kind. After giving Taylor our address we parted.

GILL: Did Taylor mention the prisoner Wilde?

PARKER: Not at that time.

GILL: Where did you first meet Wilde?

PARKER: Taylor asked us to visit him next day at Little College Street. We went the next morning. He said he could introduce us to "a man who was good for plenty of money", and that we were to meet him at the St James's bar. We went the next evening to the St James's and saw Taylor there. He took us to a restaurant in Rupert Street. I think it was the Solferino. We were shown upstairs to a private room, in which there was a dinner table laid for four. After a while Wilde came in and I was formally introduced. I had never seen him before, but I had heard of him. We dined about 8 p.m. We all four sat down to dinner, Wilde sitting on my left.

GILL: Who made the fourth?

PARKER: My brother, William Parker. I had promised Taylor that he should accompany me.

GILL: Was the dinner a good dinner?

PARKER: Yes. The table was lighted with red-shaded candles. We had plenty of champagne with our dinner and brandy and coffee afterwards. We all partook of it. Wilde paid for the dinner.

GILL: Of what nature was the conversation?

PARKER: General, at first. Nothing was then said as to the purposes for which we had come together.

GILL: And then?

PARKER: Subsequently Wilde said to me: "This is the boy for me! Will you go to the Savoy Hotel with me?" I consented, and Wilde drove me in a cab to the hotel. Only he and I went, leaving my brother and Taylor behind. At the Savoy we went first to Wilde's sitting-room on the second floor.

GILL: More drink was offered you there?

PARKER: Yes, we had liqueurs. Wilde then asked me to go into his bedroom with him.

GILL: Let us know what occurred there?

PARKER: He committed the act of sodomy upon me.

GILL: With your consent?—[Parker did not reply.]—Did Wilde give you any money on that occasion?

PARKER: Before I left Wilde gave me £2, telling me to call at the Savoy Hotel in a week. I went there about a week afterwards at 11 p.m. We had supper, with champagne. Wilde on that occasion committed the same acts as on the first occasion. I stayed about two hours. When I left, Wilde gave me £3. I remember subsequently going with my brother to 13 Little College Street. We slept there with Taylor. Taylor told us on that occasion that he had gone through a form of marriage with a youth named Mason.

GILL: Did he say who acted as the woman?

PARKER: Yes; he said he did; that he was in woman's dress, and that they had a wedding break-fast. ... I stayed with Taylor at Chapel Street for about a fortnight. Wilde used to call there, and the same thing occurred as at the Savoy. I had for a fortnight or three weeks a room at 50 Park Walk, Chelsea. At the time I was living at Park Walk, Wilde visited me there. I was asked by Wilde to imagine that I was a woman and that he was my lover. I had to keep up this illusion. I used to sit on his knees and he used to ...[censored] as a man might amuse himself with a girl. Wilde insisted on this filthy make-believe being kept up. Wilde visited me at Park Walk one night between 11.30 and 12. He came in a cab, and drove away after staying about a quarter of an hour. Wilde kept his cab standing outside. In consequence of this incident my landlady gave me notice to leave and I left.

GILL: Apart from money, did Wilde give you any presents?

PARKER: Yes, he gave me a silver cigarette case and a gold ring. I don't suppose boys are different to girls in acquiring presents from them who are fond of them.

GILL: You pawned the cigarette case and the ring?

PARKER: Yes.

GILL: Where else did you visit Wilde?

PARKER: I visited Wilde at his rooms in St James's Place. Taylor gave me the address. Wilde had a bedroom and a sitting-room opening into each other. I have been there in the morning and to tea in the afternoon. [Parker described a sexual act which he said took place with Wilde on one of these occasions.]

GILL: Where else have you been with Wilde?

PARKER: To Kettner's Restaurant.

GILL: What happened there?

PARKER: We dined there. We always had a lot of wine. Wilde would talk of poetry and art during dinner, and of the old Roman days.

GILL: On one occasion you proceeded from Kettner's to Wilde's house?

PARKER: Yes. We went to Tite Street. It was very late at night. Wilde let himself and me in with a latchkey. I remained the night, sleeping with the prisoner, and he himself let me out in the early morning before anyone was about.

GILL: Where else have you visited this man?

PARKER: At the Albemarle Hotel. The same thing happened there.

GILL: Where did your last interview take place?

PARKER: I last saw Wilde in Trafalgar Square about nine months ago. He was in a hansom and saw me. He alighted from the hansom and spoke to me.

GILL: What did he say?

PARKER: He asked me how I was and said: "Well, you are looking as pretty as ever." He did not ask me to go anywhere with him then.

GILL: During the period of your acquaintance with Wilde did you frequently see Taylor?

PARKER: Yes.

GILL: Who else did you meet at Little College Street?

PARKER: Atkins, Wood, and Scarfe, amongst others.

GILL: Did you continue your acquaintance with Taylor until a certain incident occurred last

August? You were arrested in the course of a police raid on a certain house in Fitzroy Street?

PARKER: Yes.

GILL: Orgies of the most disgraceful kind used to happen there?

PARKER: Yes.

MR J. P. GRAIN [attorney for Taylor]: My lord, I must protest against the introduction of matter extraneous to the indictment. Surely I have enough to answer.

GILL: I wish to show that Parker ceased his acquaintance with Taylor after that incident. When did you cease your association with Taylor?

PARKER: In August 1894. I went away into the country and took up another occupation.

MR JUSTICE CHARLES: What was the occupation?

PARKER: I enlisted. While I was with my regiment I was seen by Lord Queensberry's solicitor, and he took down a statement from me.

GILL: Until you became acquainted with Taylor had you ever been mixed up with men in the commission of indecent acts?

PARKER: No, never.

Cross-examination by Sir Edward Clarke

CLARKE: On what date did you enlist?

PARKER: On 3 September.

CLARKE: When were you seen in the country in reference to this case?

PARKER: Towards the end of March.

CLARKE: Did you state at Bow Street that you received £30 not to say anything about a certain case?

PARKER: Yes. I stated at the Police Court that I had received £30, part of moneys extorted from a gentleman with whom I had committed acts of indecency. I received the £30 a few days before I was arrested in August 1894. I can't remember the exact date, but it was a month or two before I enlisted.

CLARKE: I don't ask the name of the gentleman from whom the money was extorted, but I do ask the names of the two men who got the money and gave you £30?

PARKER: Wood and Allen. I could not tell you where Allen is now. He used to live in Crawford Street. Wood is a witness in this case, I know.

CLARKE: When had the incident occurred in consequence of which you received the £30—how long before?

PARKER: I cannot think.

CLARKE: You had had indecent behaviour with the gentleman in question?

PARKER: Yes, but only on one occasion, at Camera Square, Chelsea.

CLARKE: Where you were living?

PARKER: Yes.

CLARKE: Did the gentleman come to your room?

PARKER: Yes.

CLARKE: By your invitation?

PARKER: He asked me if he could come.

CLARKE: And you took him home with you?

PARKER: Yes.

CLARKE: Did Wood and Allen happen to come in while the gentleman was there?

PARKER: No.

CLARKE: How much did Wood and Allen tell you they got?

PARKER: I can't remember.

CLARKE: Try and remember?

PARKER: £300 or £400.

CLARKE: Was that the first sum of money you had received under circumstances of that kind?

PARKER: Yes.

CLARKE: What did you do with the £30?

PARKER: Spent it.

CLARKE: And then went into the army?

PARKER: I spent it in about a couple of days.

CLARKE: I'll leave that question. You say positively that Mr Wilde committed sodomy with you at the Savoy?

PARKER: Yes.

CLARKE: But you have been in the habit of accusing other gentlemen of the same offence?

PARKER: Never, unless it has been done.

CLARKE: I submit that you blackmail gentlemen?

PARKER: No, sir. I have accepted money, but it has been offered to me to pay me for the offence. I have been solicited. I have never suggested this offence to gentlemen. . . .

CLARKE: When you allowed yourself to be introduced to Mr Wilde, you knew perfectly well the purpose for which the introduction was made?

PARKER: Yes.

CLARKE: At the dinner, Mr Wilde was the principal conversationalist, I suppose?

PARKER: Yes.

CLARKE: And you found him a brilliant and an amusing talker?

PARKER: Yes.

CLARKE: Was the door locked during the time you describe?

PARKER: On the first visit to the Savoy Hotel Wilde locked the bedroom door. I did not see any servants as I left the hotel. I went away in a hansom. As to the second visit, Wilde told me the night and the time to come again. I found Wilde occupying the same rooms. I gave my name and the hall porter showed me up by the lift. Wilde on this occasion, too, locked the bedroom door. The waiter who served the supper of course saw me there. It was on the second or third floor; I cannot be certain which. In the sitting-room Mr Wilde rang a bell for the waiter, and the waiter went for drinks and brought them in. The sitting-room and bedroom opened one into the other. Mr Wilde did not lock the sitting-room door, but he locked that of the bedroom. I did not know Mr Wilde even by sight till I was introduced to him at the restaurant. I did not see anybody but a hall boy at the hotel entrance.

CLARKE: There was no concealment about your

visit, was there? You gave your name, were shown up, and in going away you did not attempt to avoid any of the servants?

PARKER: That's so.

CLARKE: Did you hear that Wood had got £20 or £30 from Mr Wilde for some letters?

PARKER: I did not hear that he got the money. I heard from someone, I can't remember from whom, that Wood got the letters out of some clothes which were given to him by Lord Alfred Douglas. I never saw the letters.

CLARKE: Were Wilde's rooms on the ground floor at St James's Place very public ones?

PARKER: Yes. There were men servants about. The sitting-room was a sort of library. There were a good many books about.

CLARKE: Do you suggest that in rooms such as you have described and so situated this kind of conduct went on again and again?

PARKER: Yes.

CLARKE: There was not the smallest concealment about your visit with Mr Wilde to the music-hall?

PARKER: No.

CLARKE: You shared a box with him at the Pavilion?

PARKER: Yes.

Re-examination by Mr Charles Gill

GILL: Did you know Lord Alfred Douglas?

PARKER: Yes. Taylor introduced me to him. I know that the letters referred to belonged to Lord Alfred Douglas. Until I met Taylor I did not know Atkins, Wood, Allen, Cliburn, or Burton.

GILL: When did you first make the acquaintance of Wood?

PARKER: About six months before he went to America.

TESTIMONY OF PROSECUTION WITNESS ALFRED WOOD

Examination by Mr Horace Avory

WOOD: I was formerly a clerk. In January 1893 I was not in any occupation. I first knew Taylor about that time.

AVORY: When did you go to Little College Street to live?

WOOD: In January 1893. I stayed there about three weeks.

AVORY: Where did you sleep there?

WOOD: In the same room with Taylor. There was only one bed there.

AVORY: When did you first get to know Wilde?

WOOD: About a month after I made the acquaintance of Taylor.

AVORY: How did you come to know Wilde?

WOOD: I was introduced to him by a gentleman at the Café Royal.

AVORY: Who was the gentleman?

WOOD: Must I give the name?

AVORY: Yes.

WOOD: Lord Alfred Douglas.

AVORY: What took place when you were introduced to Wilde?

WOOD: Mr Wilde was sitting down. He spoke to me first. He asked: "Are you Alfred Wood?" I said: "Yes". Then he offered me something to drink and I had something; and then he invited me to go round to the Florence in Rupert Street for dinner. I went with him and we dined in a private room.

AVORY: What kind of meal was it?

WOOD: Very nice, one of the best to be got.

AVORY: What wine did you have?

WOOD: Champagne. After dinner I went with Mr Wilde to 16 Tite Street. There was nobody in the house to my knowledge. Mr Wilde let himself in with a latchkey. We went up to a bedroom where we had hock and seltzer. Here an act of grossest indecency occurred. Mr Wilde used his influence to induce me to consent. He made me nearly drunk.—[Censored]—Afterwards I lay on the sofa with him. It was a long time, however, before I would allow him to actually do the act of indecency.

AVORY: Did he give you any money that night?

WOOD: Yes, at the Florence. About £3 I think it was. He said he thought I must need some money to buy some things with. The money was given me before any suggestion about going to Tite Street. ...

AVORY: Did you ever meet Wilde again?

WOOD: He once came to my room in Langham Street.

AVORY: Did you know he was coming?

WOOD: Yes.

AVORY: How did you know?

WOOD: He came by appointment. He took me out to buy a present. He bought me a half-dozen shirts, some collars and handkerchiefs, and a silver watch and chain. Before he took me out we had some tea.

AVORY: Up to what time did your acquaintance-ship with Wilde go on?

WOOD: Up to the end of March.

AVORY: How did it cease?

WOOD: I told Mr Taylor that I would like to get away from a certain class of people. I think I men-tioned it to Mr Wilde, who gave me £30. I saw him at Taylor's rooms.

AVORY: What took place between you?

WOOD: Mr Wilde asked me if I wanted to go away to America. I said, "Yes", and then he said he would give me the money. He said, "You have some let-ters I should like to get back", and he gave me £30.

AVORY: Was it a fact that you had any letters of his in your possession?

WOOD: Yes. I don't remember how many.

AVORY: Did the letters belong to you?

WOOD: No. They were letters I found in some clothes Lord Alfred Douglas had given me. They were letters from Mr Wilde to Lord Alfred Douglas.

TESTIMONY OF PROSECUTION WITNESS EDWARD SHELLEY

Examination by Mr Horace Avory

SHELLEY: I am 21 years of age. In 1891 I was employed as a clerk in the offices of Messrs Elkin Mathews & John Lane, publishers, of the Bodley Head, Vigo Street, W. In 1892 they were publishing a book for Mr Wilde. Mr Wilde was in the habit of coming to the firm's place of business; he seemed to take note of me, and he generally stopped and spoke to me for a few moments. As Mr Wilde was leaving Vigo Street one day he invited me to dine with him at the Albemarle Hotel. I kept the appointment. I was proud of the invitation. We dined together in a public room. Mr Wilde was very kind and attentive and pressed me to drink. I had champagne with dinner, and after had whisky and soda and smoked cigarettes in Mr Wilde's sitting-room.

AVORY: What happened afterwards?

SHELLEY: I do not like to say. ... Mr Wilde's conversation was principally about books and myself. Mr Wilde said: "Will you come into my bedroom?" I did not know what he meant. As I went into the room Mr Wilde kissed me. He also put his arms round me. I had been taking a lot of wine. I felt insulted, degraded, and objected vigorously. Mr Wilde said he was sorry and that he had drunk too much wine. I stayed the night and shared his bed. Mr Wilde saw me next day and again kissed me and there was a repetition of the previous night's performance. Mr Wilde said he could get me on, and he invited me to go with him to Brighton, Cromer, and Paris, but I did not go. He made me a present of a set of his writings, including *The Picture of Dorian Gray*. He wrote something in the books, "To one I like well", or something to that effect, but I tore out the pages bearing the inscriptions. I only did that quite recently, after I heard of the charges suggested by Lord Queensberry. My father objected to my friendship with Mr Wilde. At first I thought that Mr Wilde was a kind of philanthropist, fond of youth and eager to be of assistance to young men of any promise. But certain speeches and actions on the part of Mr Wilde caused me to alter this opinion. I also received letters from Mr Wilde which I kept until about a couple of years ago. At the same time I wrote Mr Wilde a letter in which I said that I could not have anything more to do with a man of his morality and that I would break off the acquaintance.

Cross-examination by Sir Edward Clarke

CLARKE: About two years ago, in 1893, did you write a certain letter to Mr Wilde?

SHELLEY: Yes.

CLARKE: On what subject?

SHELLEY: It was to break off the acquaintance.

CLARKE: How did the letter begin?

SHELLEY: It began "Sir".

CLARKE: Give me the gist of it?

SHELLEY: I believe I said: "I have suffered more from my acquaintance with you than you are ever likely to know of." I further said that he was an immoral man and that I would never, if I could help it, see him again.

CLARKE: If such a thing as you allege happened you must have resented the outrage upon you?

SHELLEY: Yes, I did.

CLARKE: Then why did you go and dine with him the very next day?

SHELLEY: I suppose I was a young fool. I tried to think the best of him.

CLARKE: Are you sure that you have not made any mistake with reference to what you say occurred between you and Mr Wilde?

SHELLEY: No, I have made no mistake.

CLARKE: Did it occur to you after the second occasion that it was a sin?

SHELLEY: Yes, it did occur to me that it was a sin I was committing.

CLARKE: Did you become familiar with some of Mr Wilde's writings?

SHELLEY: Yes.

CLARKE: And did you talk to him upon literary subjects?

SHELLEY: Yes, before I went to the Albemarle Hotel.

CLARKE: You seem to have put the worst possible construction on his liking for you. Did your friendly relations with Mr Wilde remain unbroken until the time you wrote that letter in March 1893?

SHELLEY: Yes.

CLARKE: Have you seen Mr Wilde since then?

SHELLEY: Yes.

CLARKE: After that letter?

SHELLEY: Yes.

CLARKE: Where did you see him?

SHELLEY: I went to see him in Tite Street.

CLARKE [reading from a letter written by Shelley to Wilde after the commission of the alleged acts]:

> Dear Oscar ... I can never forget your kindness and
> am conscious that I can never sufficiently express my
> thankfulness to you. ...

CLARKE: Was it present in your mind at the time you wrote this that Mr Wilde had insulted you when you had had too much to drink?

SHELLEY: Certainly, I could not forget such a thing.

CLARKE: Were you under the painful sense of having committed sin?

SHELLEY: I tried to forget it. I wanted to think some good of the man. I thought Mr Wilde was really sorry for what he had done.

CLARKE: What do you mean, "for what he had done"?

SHELLEY: His improper behaviour with young men.

CLARKE: Yet you say he never practised any actual improprieties upon you?

SHELLEY: Because he saw that I would never allow anything of the kind. He did not disguise from me what he wanted, or what his usual customs with young men were.

CLARKE: Yet you wrote him grateful letters breathing apparent friendship?

SHELLEY: For the reason I have given.

CLARKE: These letters were written to one whom you thought an immoral man?

SHELLEY: Yes.

CLARKE: Well, we'll leave that question. Now, tell me why did you leave the Vigo Street firm of publishers?

SHELLEY: Because it got to be known that I was friendly with Oscar Wilde.

CLARKE: Did you leave the firm of your own accord?

SHELLEY: Yes.

CLARKE: Why?

SHELLEY: People employed there, my fellow clerks, chaffed me about my acquaintance with Mr Wilde.

CLARKE: In what way?

SHELLEY: They implied scandalous things. They called me "Mrs Wilde" and "Miss Oscar".

CLARKE: So you left?

SHELLEY: I resolved to put an end to an intolerable position.

CLARKE: You were in bad odour at home too, I think?

SHELLEY: Yes, a little.

CLARKE: I put it to you that your father requested you to leave his house?

SHELLEY: Yes. He strongly objected to my friendship with Mr Wilde. But the difference between us was made up again.

CLARKE: I find that in January of this year you were in serious trouble?

SHELLEY: In what way?

CLARKE: You were arrested for an assault upon your father?

SHELLEY: Yes, I was.

CLARKE: Did your father tell you to leave his house?

SHELLEY: Yes. It was because of my friendship with Mr Wilde.

CLARKE: Did your parents accuse you of idleness?

SHELLEY: Yes, they thought me idle.

CLARKE: Were you quite in your sound mind when you assaulted your father?

SHELLEY: No, I couldn't have been.

CLARKE: Where were you taken?

SHELLEY: To the Fulham Police Station.

CLARKE: You were offered bail?

SHELLEY: Yes.

CLARKE: Did you send to Mr Wilde and ask him to bail you out?

SHELLEY: Yes.

CLARKE: What happened?

SHELLEY: In an hour my father went to the station and I was liberated. My father withdrew the charge and the case was dismissed.

TESTIMONY OF PROSECUTION WITNESS ANTONIO MIGGE

Examination by Mr Charles Gill

MIGGE: I am a professor of massage, and I attend the Savoy Hotel to massage patients. I attended to massage Mr Oscar Wilde at the hotel, a bedroom on the third floor being occupied by him. It was March 1893, from the 16th to the 20th of the month. One morning on going into the room—I entered after knocking—I saw someone in bed. At first I thought it was a young lady, as I saw only the head, but afterwards I saw that it was a young man. It was someone about 16 to 18 years of age. Mr Wilde was in the same room dressing himself. He told me he felt so much better that morning and that, as he was very busy, he could not stay to have the treatment. I never attended Mr Wilde again.

Cross-examination by Sir Edward Clarke

CLARKE: You had gone to the room at the usual time for the massage, had you not?

MIGGE: Yes.

CLARKE: Was the door of the bedroom locked?

MIGGE: No, the door was not locked.

CLARKE: And when you opened the door, Mr Wilde was dressing?

MIGGE: Yes.

CLARKE: In what part of the room was he?

MIGGE: At the washstand.

TESTIMONY OF PROSECUTION WITNESS JANE COTTER

Examination by Mr Horace Avory

COTTER: I am employed as a chambermaid in the Savoy Hotel. I remember Mr Wilde staying at the hotel in March 1893. At first he occupied No. 361 and Lord Douglas the room adjoining, No. 362. I found it necessary to call the attention of the housekeeper to the condition of Mr Wilde's bed. The sheets were stained in a peculiar way. On the third morning of his stay, about 11 a.m., Mr Wilde rang the bell for the housemaid. On answering the bell I met Mr Wilde in the doorway of No. 361, and he told me he wanted a fire in his own room, No. 362. There I saw a boy of 18 or 19 years of age with dark close-cropped hair and a sallow complexion. Some days later Lord Alfred Douglas left the hotel, and Mr Wilde then removed into rooms in the front of the hotel.

TESTIMONY OF DEFENCE WITNESS OSCAR WILDE

Examination by Sir Edward Clarke

WILDE: In 1884 I married Miss Constance Lloyd, and from that time to the present I have lived with her at 16 Tite Street, Chelsea. I have occupied also for a time some rooms at St James's Place, which I took for the purpose of my literary work, it being quite out of the question to secure quiet and mental repose at my own house when my two young sons were at home. I have heard the evidence against me in this case, and I declare that there is no truth in any one of the allegations of indecent behaviour.

CLARKE: Was the evidence you gave [in the libel trial] absolutely and in all respects true?

WILDE: Entirely true evidence.

CLARKE: Is there any truth in any of the allegations made against you in the evidence in this case?

WILDE: There is no truth whatsoever in any one of the allegations, no truth whatsoever.

Cross-examination by Mr Charles Gill

GILL: You are acquainted with a publication entitled *The Chameleon*?

WILDE: Very well indeed.

GILL: Contributors to that journal are friends of yours?

WILDE: That is so.

GILL: I believe that Lord Alfred Douglas was a frequent contributor?

WILDE: Hardly that, I think. He wrote some verses occasionally for *The Chameleon*, and indeed for other papers.

GILL: The poems in question were somewhat peculiar?

WILDE: They certainly were not mere commonplaces like so much that is labelled poetry.

GILL: The tone of them met with your critical approval?

WILDE: It was not for me to approve or disapprove. I left that to the reviews.

GILL: On the last occasion you were cross-examined

with reference to two letters written to Lord Alfred Douglas?

WILDE: Yes.

GILL: You were asked as to those letters, as to *The Picture of Dorian Gray* and as to *The Chameleon*?

WILDE: Yes.

GILL: You said you had read Lord Alfred Douglas's poems in *The Chameleon*?

WILDE: Yes.

GILL: You described them as beautiful poems?

WILDE: I said something tantamount to that. The verses were original in theme and construction, and I admired them.

GILL: Lord Alfred Douglas contributed two poems to *The Chameleon*, and they were beautiful poems?

WILDE: Yes.

GILL: Listen, Mr Wilde, I shall keep you only a very short time in the witness box. [Gill read the following poem from *The Chameleon*.]

> Last night unto my bed methought there came
> Our lady of strange dreams, and from an urn
> She poured live fire, so that mine eyes did burn
> At sight of it. Anon the floating flame
> Took many shapes, and one cried: "I am Shame
> That walks with Love, I am most wise to turn

Cold lips and limbs to fire; therefore discern
And see my loveliness, and praise my name."

And afterwards, in radiant garments dressed
With sound of flutes and laughing of glad lips,
A pomp of all the passions passed along
All the night through; till the white phantom ships
Of dawn sailed in. Whereat I said this song,
"Of all sweet passions Shame is loveliest."

GILL: Is that one of the beautiful poems?

SIR EDWARD CLARKE: That is not one of Mr Wilde's.

GILL: I am not aware that I said it was.

CLARKE: I thought you would be glad to say it was not.

MR JUSTICE CHARLES: I understand that was a poem by Lord Alfred Douglas.

GILL: Yes, my lord, and one which the witness described as a beautiful poem. The other beautiful poem is the one that follows immediately and precedes "The Priest and the Acolyte".

GILL: Your view, Mr Wilde, is that the "shame" mentioned here is that shame which is a sense of modesty?

WILDE: That was the explanation given to me by the person who wrote it. The sonnet seemed to me obscure.

GILL: During 1893 and 1894 you were a good deal in the company of Lord Alfred Douglas?

WILDE: Oh, yes.

GILL: Did he read that poem to you?

WILDE: Yes.

GILL: You can, perhaps, understand that such verses as these would not be acceptable to the reader with an ordinarily balanced mind?

WILDE: I am not prepared to say. It appears to me to be a question of taste, temperament, and individuality. I should say that one man's poetry is another man's poison!—[Laughter]—

GILL: I daresay! The next poem is one described as *Two Loves*. It contains these lines:

> "Sweet youth,
> Tell me why, sad and sighing, thou dost rove
> These pleasant realms? I pray thee tell me sooth,
> What is thy name?" He said, "My name is Love."
> Then straight the first did turn himself to me,
> And cried, "He lieth, for his name is Shame.
> But I am Love, and I was wont to be
> Alone in this fair garden, till he came
> Unasked by night; I am true Love, I fill
> The hearts of boy and girl with mutual flame."
> Then sighing, said the other, "Have thy will,
> I am the love that dare not speak its name."

GILL: Was that poem explained to you?

WILDE: I think that is clear.

GILL: There is no question as to what it means?

WILDE: Most certainly not.

GILL: Is it not clear that the love described relates to natural love and unnatural love?

WILDE: No.

GILL: What is the "love that dare not speak its name"?

WILDE: The "love that dare not speak its name" in this century is such a great affection of an elder for a younger man as there was between David and Jonathan, such as Plato made the very basis of his philosophy, and such as you find in the sonnets of Michelangelo and Shakespeare. It is that deep, spiritual affection that is as pure as it is perfect. It dictates and pervades great works of art like those of Shakespeare and Michelangelo, and those two letters of mine, such as they are. It is in this century misunderstood, so much misunderstood that it may be described as the "love that dare not speak its name", and on account of it I am placed where I am now. It is beautiful, it is fine, it is the noblest form of affection. There is nothing unnatural about it. It is intellectual, and it repeatedly exists between an elder and a younger man, when the elder man has intellect, and the younger man has all the joy, hope, and glamour of life before him. That it should be so the world does not understand. The world mocks at it and sometimes puts one in the pillory for it.—[Loud applause, mingled with some hisses]—

MR JUSTICE CHARLES: If there is the slightest manifestation of feeling I shall have the Court cleared. There must be complete silence preserved.

GILL: Then there is no reason why it should be called "Shame"?

WILDE: Ah, that, you will see, is the mockery of the other love—love which is jealous of friendship and says to it, "You should not interfere".

GILL: You were staying at the Savoy Hotel with Lord Alfred Douglas at the beginning of March 1893?

WILDE: Yes.

GILL: And after that you went into rooms?

WILDE: Yes.

GILL: I understand you to say that the evidence given in this case by the witnesses called in support of the prosecution is absolutely untrue?

WILDE: Entirely.

GILL: Entirely untrue?

WILDE: Yes.

GILL: Did you hear the evidence of the servants from the Savoy?

WILDE: It is absolutely untrue.

GILL: Had you a quarrel with Lord Alfred Douglas in that week?

WILDE: No; we never did quarrel—perhaps a little difference. Sometimes he said things that pained me and sometimes I said things that pained him.

GILL: Had he that week said unkind things?

WILDE: I always made a point of forgetting whenever he said anything unkind.

GILL: I wish to call your attention to the style of your correspondence with Lord Alfred Douglas?

WILDE: I am ready. I am never ashamed of the style of my writings.

GILL: You are fortunate, or shall I say shameless?— [Laughter]—I refer to passages in two letters in particular?

WILDE: Kindly quote them.

GILL: In letter number one you use the expression: "Your slim gilt soul", and you refer to Lord Alfred's "red rose-leaf lips". The second letter contains the words, "You are the divine thing I want", and describes Lord Alfred's letter as being "delightful, red and yellow wine to me". Do you think that an ordinarily constituted being would address such expressions to a younger man?

WILDE: I am not, happily I think, an ordinarily constituted being.

GILL: It is agreeable to be able to agree with you, Mr Wilde?—[Laughter]—

WILDE: There is nothing, I assure you, in either letter of which I need be ashamed. The first letter is really a prose poem, and the second more of a literary answer to one Lord Alfred had sent me.

GILL: In reference to the incidents alleged against you at the Savoy Hotel, are you prepared to contradict the evidence of the hotel servants?

WILDE: It is entirely untrue. Can I answer for what hotel servants say years after I have left the hotel? It is childish. I am not responsible for hotel servants. I have stayed at the hotel and been there constantly since.

GILL: There is no possibility of mistake? There was no woman with you?

WILDE: Certainly not.

GILL: You knew that while the counsel for Lord Queensberry was addressing the jury, the case was interrupted, a verdict of "Not Guilty" was agreed to, and the jury found that the justification was proved and the libel published for the public benefit?

WILDE: I was not in Court.

GILL: But you knew it?

WILDE: No, I did not. I knew my counsel had considered it would be impossible to get a verdict on the question as far as the literature went, and it was not for me to dispute their superior wisdom. I was not in Court, nor have I read any account of that trial.

GILL: What is there untrue in the evidence of Shelley?

WILDE: I say that his account of what happened is entirely untrue. It is true that he came to the Independent Theatre with me, but it was in a box with some friends. His accusations of impropriety are equally untrue.

GILL: Do you see no impropriety in kissing a boy?

WILDE: In kissing a young boy, a child, of course not; but I certainly do not think that one should kiss a young man of 18.

GILL: Then as to Shelley's letters, there was a line in a later one which says: "God forgive the past; do your best for me now." Do you know the meaning of that?

WILDE: Yes. Shelley was in the habit of writing me many morbid, very morbid letters, which I tore up. In them he said that he was a great sinner and anxious to be in closer communion with religion. I always tore them up.

GILL: Charles Parker—what part of his evidence is untrue?

WILDE: Where he says he came to the Savoy and that I committed acts of indecency with him. He never came to the Savoy with me to supper. It is true that he dined with me and that he came to St James's Place to tea. The rest is untrue.

GILL: Who introduced you to Wood?

WILDE: Lord Alfred Douglas.

GILL: Did you ever take Wood to Tite Street with you?

WILDE: It is entirely untrue that he ever went to Tite Street with me at all.

GILL: And these witnesses have, you say, lied throughout?

WILDE: Their evidence as to my association with them, as to the dinners taking place and the small presents I gave them, is mostly true. But there is not a particle of truth in that part of the evidence which alleged improper behaviour.

GILL: Why did you take up with these youths?

WILDE: I am a lover of youth.—[Laughter]—

GILL: You exalt youth as a sort of god?

WILDE: I like to study the young in everything. There is something fascinating in youthfulness.

GILL: So you would prefer puppies to dogs and kittens to cats?

WILDE: I think so. I should enjoy, for instance, the society of a beardless, briefless barrister quite as much as that of the most accomplished QC.—[Laughter]—

GILL: I hope the former, whom I represent in large numbers, will appreciate the compliment.—[More laughter]—These youths were much inferior to you in station?

WILDE: I never inquired, nor did I care, what station they occupied. I found them, for the most part, bright and entertaining. I found their conversation a change. It acted as a kind of mental tonic.

GILL: Who introduced you to Taylor?

WILDE: Mr Schwabe.

GILL: Why did you go to Taylor's rooms?

WILDE: Because I used to meet actors and singers of many kinds there.

GILL: A rather curious establishment, wasn't it, Taylor's?

WILDE: I didn't think so.

GILL: You saw nothing peculiar or suggestive in the arrangement of Taylor's rooms?

WILDE: I cannot say that I did. They were Bohemian. That is all. I have seen stranger rooms.

GILL: Did you notice that no one could see in through the windows?

WILDE: No; that I didn't notice.

GILL: He burned incense, did he not?

WILDE: Pastilles, I think.

GILL: Incense, I suggest?

WILDE: I think not. Pastilles, I should say, in those little Japanese things that run along rods.

GILL: Did it strike you that this place was at all peculiar?

WILDE: Not at all.

GILL: Not the sort of street you would usually visit in? You had no other friends there?

WILDE: No; this was merely a bachelor's place.

GILL: Rather a rough neighbourhood?

WILDE: That I don't know. I know it was near the Houses of Parliament.

GILL: What did you go there for?

WILDE: To amuse myself sometimes; to smoke a cigarette; for music, singing, chatting and nonsense of that kind, to while an hour away.

GILL: You never suspected the relations that might exist between Taylor and his young friends?

WILDE: I had no need to suspect anything. Taylor's relations with his friends appeared to me to be quite normal.

GILL: I may take it, Mr Wilde, that you see no reason why the police should keep observation at Little College Street?

WILDE: No.

GILL: What do you say about Alphonse Conway?

WILDE: I met him on the beach at Worthing. He was such a bright, happy boy that it was a pleasure to talk to him. I bought him a walking stick and a suit of clothes and a hat with a bright ribbon, but I was not responsible for the ribbon.—[Laughter]—

GILL: You made handsome presents to all these young fellows?

WILDE: Pardon me, I differ. I gave two or three of them a cigarette case. Boys of that class smoke a good deal of cigarettes. I have a weakness for presenting my acquaintances with cigarette cases.

GILL: Rather an expensive habit if indulged in indiscriminately, isn't it?

WILDE: Less extravagant than giving jewelled garters to ladies.—[Laughter]—

GILL: With regard to your friendship towards the persons I have mentioned, may I take it, Mr Wilde, that it was as you describe, a deep affection of an elder man for a younger?

WILDE: Certainly not. One feels that once in one's life, and once only, towards anybody.

TESTIMONY OF DEFENCE WITNESS ALFRED TAYLOR

Examination by Mr J. P. Grain

TAYLOR: I am 33 years of age. I am the son of a cocoa manufacturer, whose business is now being carried on as a limited liability company. Up to the age of 16 or 17 I was educated at Marlborough School, 2nd. Afterwards I went to a private tutor at Preston, near Brighton. I then entered the militia, going into the 4th Battalion of the Royal Fusiliers, City of London Regiment. My original intention was to go into the army, but on coming of age in

1883 I came into a fortune of £45,000 and have since that time had no occupation but have lived a life of pleasure.

Cross-examination by Mr Charles Gill

TAYLOR: I have no occupation. It is untrue that I was expelled from a public school for being caught in a compromising situation with a small boy in the lavatory. It is true that I used to have a number of young men living in my rooms and sleeping in the same bed.

GILL: Is it true that you ever went through a mock marriage with Mason?

TAYLOR: Absolutely untrue.

GILL: Had you a woman's dress in your rooms?

TAYLOR: An Eastern costume.

GILL: A woman's dress?

TAYLOR: Yes.

GILL: A woman's wig?

TAYLOR: I will explain. It was ...

GILL: Had you women's stockings?

TAYLOR: Yes.

GILL: At the time you were living in Chapel Street, were you in serious money difficulties?

TAYLOR: I had just gone through the Bankruptcy Court.

GILL: Have you not actually made a living since your bankruptcy by procuring lads and young men for rich gentlemen whom you knew to be given to this vice?

TAYLOR: No.

GILL: Have you not extracted large sums of money from wealthy men by threatening to accuse them of immoralities?

TAYLOR: No.

GILL: You made the acquaintance of the Parkers in the St James's restaurant?

TAYLOR: It was outside, and I was introduced to them by a friend.

GILL: What did you give them your address for?

TAYLOR: Well, when one makes an acquaintance and you think you will like one another ...

GILL: Are you in the habit of speaking to young men in Piccadilly?

TAYLOR: I know what you mean. No.

GILL: You go into Piccadilly?

TAYLOR: Yes, always.

GILL: St James's?

TAYLOR: Yes.

GILL: Have you ever accosted men at the Alhambra or the Empire?

TAYLOR: Never.

GILL: Did you know Mr Wilde well?

TAYLOR: Yes.

GILL: Did you tell certain lads that he was fond of boys?

TAYLOR: No, never.

GILL: Did you know that he is?

TAYLOR: I believe he is fond of young people.

GILL: Why did you introduce Charles Parker to Mr Wilde?

TAYLOR: I thought Mr Wilde might use his influence to obtain for him some work on the stage.

GILL: Did you know a man named Marling who was concerned in the Fitzroy Street raid?

TAYLOR: Yes.

GILL: Do you know what he is?

TAYLOR: I have heard a good deal.

GILL: Were you and Charles Parker both arrested in that raid?

TAYLOR: Yes, but we were discharged from custody.

GILL: What was the reason for the dinner at Kettner's?

TAYLOR: It was in honour of my birthday. After dinner was over the Parkers and I went home to my rooms in Little College Street.

GILL: Why did you burn incense in your rooms?

TAYLOR: Because I liked it.

TRANSCRIPT EXCERPTS FROM
THE SECOND CRIMINAL TRIAL

After three weeks of freedom, Wilde reappeared at the Old Bailey on 20 May 1895, again defended by Sir Edward Clarke. This time the prosecution was led by Solicitor-General Frank Lockwood. The second criminal trial closely followed the first, apart from the fact that the prosecution dropped the weakest witnesses and focused more heavily on the strongest. Therefore only excerpts from the speeches from the closing part of the trial are included here.

CLOSING SPEECH FOR THE DEFENCE

SIR EDWARD CLARKE: May it please you, my lord, gentlemen of the jury. Having in my mind the observations which, under some stress of feeling I made in the early part of the day, I may state at the outset that I recognise the admirable fairness with which the Solicitor-General cross-examined Mr Wilde. And if earlier in the day I was moved, by what I am glad to think I then described as the momentary forgetfulness of my learned friend yesterday, to expressions which sounded hostile in regard to him, he will let me say at once, in the frankest manner, that the way in which he has cross-examined absolutely destroys any suggestion which might have lain in my words. . . .

I suggest to you, gentlemen, that your duty is simple and clear and that when you find a man who is assailed by tainted evidence entering the witness-box, and for a third time giving a clear, coherent, and lucid account of the transactions, such as that which the accused has given today, I venture to say that that man is entitled to be believed against a horde of blackmailers such as you have seen [in] this matter. I know not on what grounds the course has been taken. . . .

This trial seems to be operating as an act of indemnity for all the blackmailers in London. Wood and Parker, in giving evidence, have established for themselves a sort of statute of limitations.

In testifying on behalf of the Crown they have secured immunity for past rogueries and indecencies. It is on the evidence of Parker and Wood that you are asked to condemn Mr Wilde. And Mr Wilde knew nothing of the characters of these men. They were introduced to him, and it was his love of admiration that caused him to be in their society. The positions should really be changed. It is these men who ought to be the accused, not the accusers. It is true that Charles Parker and Wood never made any charge against Mr Wilde before the plea of justification in the libel case was put in—but what a powerful piece of evidence that is in favour of Mr Wilde! For if Charles Parker and Wood thought they had material for making a charge against Mr Wilde before that date, do you not think, gentlemen, they would have made it?

Do you think that they would have remained year after year without trying to get something from him? But Charles Parker and Wood previously made no charge against Mr Wilde, nor did they attempt to get money from him, and that circumstance is one among other cogent proofs to be found in the case that there is no truth whatever in the accusations against Mr Wilde. . . .

You must not act upon suspicion or prejudice, but upon an examination of the facts, gentlemen, and on the facts, I respectfully urge that Mr Wilde is entitled to claim from you a verdict of acquittal. If on an examination of the evidence you, therefore, feel it your duty to say that the charges against the prisoner have not been proved, then I am sure that you will be glad that the brilliant promise which has been clouded by these accusations, and the bright reputation which was so nearly quenched in the torrent of prejudice which a few weeks ago was sweeping through the press, have been saved by your verdict from absolute ruin; and that it leaves him, a distinguished man of letters and a brilliant Irishman, to live among us a life of honour and repute, and to give in the maturity of his genius gifts to our literature, of which he has given only the promise in his early youth.

CLOSING SPEECH FOR THE PROSECUTION

SOLICITOR-GENERAL LOCKWOOD: As regards the hardship which my learned friend alleges to have been inflicted on the defendant in being cross-examined three times, I am prepared to argue that so far from being placed at a disadvantage, there are good grounds for coming to the conclusion that he is now better fitted and readier with his answers than before. ... It is upon the evidence only that I ask you to condemn the accused; but you will not appreciate the evidence until you know what manner of man it is you are dealing with. Who were his associates? He is a man of culture and literary tastes, and I submit that his associates ought to have been his equals and not these illiterate boys whom you have heard in the witness-box. . . .

You cannot fail to put the interpretation on the conduct of the prisoner that he is a guilty man, and you ought to say so by your verdict.

As to the statement of Sir Edward Clarke that Mr Wilde himself created inquiry into the matter: that statement of my learned friend makes it necessary for me to recall to your minds, gentlemen, the relative positions of the parties in the Queensberry case. Sir Edward Clarke has contended that Lord Queensberry's libels referred to events of two years back, and that in the lapse of time witnesses for Mr Wilde have been lost sight of. But I ask you, what witness has been lost sight of? I suggest to you that it was the fact that Wilde had seen nothing of Parker, and that he could rely implicitly on his intimate friend Taylor, that encouraged him to prosecute Lord Queensberry.

SIR EDWARD CLARKE: I must rise to object to Mr Solicitor-General's rhetorical descriptions of what has never been proved in evidence, in asserting that an intimate friendship existed between Mr Wilde and Taylor.

LOCKWOOD: Gentlemen, it is not rhetoric; it is a plain statement of fact. What are the indications of an intimate friendship? They call each other by their Christian names. Is he not a great friend on his own profession? Does he not say to Taylor: "Bring your friends; they are my friends; I will not inquire too closely whether they come from the stables or the kitchen"? No doubt my learned friend desires now to disconnect them. He wishes as a result of this trial that one should be condemned and the other left free to continue his grand literary career.

CLARKE: I protest.

LOCKWOOD: My friend hopes to preserve Wilde by means of a false glamour of art.

CLARKE: My lord, I must protest against this line of argument. I protest strongly against the line the learned Solicitor-General is taking.

LOCKWOOD: Oh, you may protest.

MR JUSTICE WILLS: So far no mention has been made of the verdict in the other case.

CLARKE: All this is as far removed from the evidence as anything ever heard in this Court.

LOCKWOOD: I am alluding, my lord, and I maintain that I am right in alluding, to my learned friend's last appeal to the jury as to the literary position of his client; and I am dealing in connection with that with his connection with the man Taylor, and I say that these men must be judged equally.

CLARKE: They ought to have been fairly tried in their proper order.

LOCKWOOD: Oh, my lord, these interruptions should avail my friend nothing.

MR JUSTICE WILLS: Mr Solicitor-General is perfectly within his rights. The only objection is to allusions to the result of the trial of Taylor.

LOCKWOOD: My learned friend does not seem to have gained a great deal by his superfluity of interruption.—[Laughter]—

MR JUSTICE WILLS: These interruptions are offensive to me beyond anything that can be described. To have to try a case of this kind, to keep the scales even and do one's duty is hard enough; but to be pestered with the applause or expressions of feeling of senseless people who have no business to be here at all except for the gratification of morbid curiosity is too much. I hope that no further interruption of this kind will be heard throughout the rest of the trial. If there is anything of the kind again I shall clear the Court.

LOCKWOOD: I contend that such a letter found in the possession of a woman from a man would be open to but one interpretation. How much worse is the inference to be drawn when such a letter is written from one man to another. It has been attempted to show that this was a prose poem, a sonnet, a lovely thing which I suppose we are too low to appreciate. Gentlemen, let us thank God, if it is so, that we do not appreciate things of this sort at their proper value, and that is somewhat lower than the beasts. If that letter had been seen by any right-minded man, it would have been looked upon as evidence of a guilty passion. And you, men of pride, reason and honour, are tried to be put off with this story of the prose poem, of the sonnet, of the lovely thing.

It is a common-sense conclusion that Mr Wilde bargained with Wood and bought the letters. Indeed Mr Wilde's own admissions—which agree up to a certain point with the evidence of Wood— prove Wood's story to be true. What necessity was there for Mr Wilde to give Wood supper in a private room or to tell him that his family was out of town? If what Mr Wilde has said is true as to his first meeting with Wood, all he had to do was to hand over to him the money he was deputed to give him and, if he thought there was aught in this young man that appealed to his own benevolence, to add such sum as provided for such refreshment as Wood might desire. In my submission Wood has no motive for deceiving you on this occasion. I say that the transaction with regard to the letters is capable of one construction only. Mr Wilde knew they were letters which he must recover; he bought them and tore them to pieces. He kept the one which he had from Allen, because he knew that Mr Beerbohm Tree had a copy of it, so that it was useless to destroy the original. Gentlemen, if you come to the conclusion that Mr Wilde did purchase these letters, it throws a flood of light upon his conduct. It shows that he knew the class of men with whom he had been intimate and with whom he continued to be intimate. . . .

My learned friend has said that these witnesses are blackmailers and has warned you against giving a verdict which should enable this detestable trade to rear its head unblushingly in this city. Gentlemen, I should have as much right to ask you to take care lest by your verdict you should enable another vice, as detestable, as abominable, to raise its head with unblushing effrontery in this city. The genesis of the blackmailer is the man who has committed these acts of indecency with him. And the genesis of the man who commits these foul acts is the man who is willing to pay for their commission. Were it not that there are men willing to purchase vice in this most hideous and detestable form, there would be no market for such crime, and no opening for these blackmailers to ply their calling. . . .

With regard to Taylor, who on the occasion of the first trial was charged by Mr Carson with procuration on behalf of Wilde, I must point out that Taylor was in Court during the Queensberry trial, and yet he was not put into the witness-box. Again, one would have thought that, after the Wood incident, Taylor would have been asked to be careful in the selection of the friends he introduced to Mr Wilde. But, no. Taylor had carte blanche to bring along any friends he pleased. He brought along Charles Parker, and it is manifest that the prisoner's intimacy with Charles Parker was not a matter of ordinary friendship. In connection with Parker's testimony I must repel the suggestion that Mr Russell, Lord Queensberry's solicitor, or any of the representatives of the Crown have given either fee or reward to the youths who have given evidence in this case. All the prosecution has done has been to take precautions to prevent tampering with those witnesses, and to ensure their attendance in Court. Naturally the witnesses have been removed secretly from place to place, and I make no apology for the course the Crown has taken in this matter. Charles Parker, whose evidence gave rise to this suggestion, could not possibly have had any sinister motive in telling a story involving his own shame and to some extent his own condemnation, for it has never been shown that Parker, whatever his past conduct may have been, has attempted to extort money from Mr Wilde.

Sir Edward Clarke has exaggerated—unintentionally, of course—what his lordship said yesterday with regard to the two cases of the person or persons unknown. My learned friend made it appear as though the evidence in these cases was exceedingly slender, but as a matter of fact his lordship has left that part of the case unreservedly for your consideration, gentlemen. Now, I contend that there is ample evidence as to these particular charges. The defendant has given no explanation of the discoveries made by the employees of the hotel. It is no conclusive answer to say that Mr Wilde did everything openly. If crime were always cautious, it would always go unpunished, and it is in moments of carelessness that crime is detected. Why was Lord Alfred Douglas, who slept in the next room, not called to deny the statements of the chambermaid? I maintain that she and the other witnesses from the Savoy Hotel could have no possible object in patching up a bogus case.

There is no reason why Mr Wilde should not be cross-examined with reference to other offences. You are entitled, gentlemen, in the interests of justice, to put a common-sense interpretation upon the conditions and circumstances under which the lads outside the present case were found. . . .

Now, gentlemen, I have been through the whole of this case. I have pointed out to you its strength, and I have to ask you to do your duty in regard to it. I have already dealt with that—as I think, unfortunate—appeal which my learned friend made as to the literary past or literary future of Oscar Wilde. With that we have in this case nothing whatever to do. He has a right to be acquitted if you believe him to be an innocent man, be his lot high or low. But if, gentlemen, in your consciences you believe that he is guilty of these charges—well, then you

have only one consideration, and that is to follow closely the obligation of the oath which has
been laid upon you.

SENTENCING STATEMENT

*The following statement was read to Wilde and Taylor
after the jury returned its "Guilty" verdict.*

MR JUSTICE WILLS: Oscar Wilde and Alfred Taylor,
the crime of which you have been convicted is so
bad that one has to put stern restraint upon oneself
to prevent oneself from describing, in language
which I would rather not use, the sentiments
which must rise in the breast of every man of honour who has heard the details of these two horrible
trials. That the jury has arrived at a correct verdict
in this case I cannot persuade myself to entertain a
shadow of a doubt; and I hope, at all events, that
those who sometimes imagine that a judge is half-
hearted in the cause of decency and morality
because he takes care no prejudice shall enter into
the case, may see that it is consistent at least with
the utmost sense of indignation at the horrible
charges brought home to both of you.

It is no use for me to address you. People who
can do these things must be dead to all sense of
shame, and one cannot hope to produce any effect
upon them. It is the worst case I have ever tried.

That you, Taylor, kept a kind of male brothel it is impossible to doubt. And that you, Wilde, have been the centre of a circle of extensive corruption of the most hideous kind among young men, it is equally impossible to doubt.

I shall, under the circumstances, be expected to pass the severest sentence that the law allows. In my judgement it is totally inadequate for a case such as this. The sentence of the Court is that each of you be imprisoned and kept to hard labour for two years.—[Cries of "Oh! Oh!" and "Shame!"]—

WILDE: And I? May I say nothing, my Lord?

The Court adjourned.

∞⋘⋙∞

Oscar Wilde served two years at hard labour. On his release from Reading Gaol he travelled in Europe, relying on the benevolence of friends. He died on 30 November 1900 in Paris, aged 46. De Profundis, the abridged version of a 30,000-word letter Wilde wrote to Douglas from prison, was published in 1905.

New titles in the series

The Compendiums

Each book in this handsome series consists of three key historical accounts, and is illustrated with maps and photographs.

The World War I Collection

The official inquiry into the disastrous military campaign at Gallipoli, plus the despatches of British generals at the front during the first nine months of the war, are presented here.
The Dardanelles Commission, 1914–16
Examines why, when British troops were already heavily deployed in France, the leaders of the day saw fit to launch a major offensive in the eastern Mediterranean.
British Battles of World War I, 1914–15
A collection of despatches written by British commanders in the field, mainly in northern France.

ISBN 0 11 702466 X   Price UK £14.99 US $19.95

The World War II Collection

Consists of three accounts of major milestones of World War II, written by the statesmen and military leaders of the day.
War 1939: Dealing with Adolf Hitler
Describes the policies of both Hitler and the British government in the months leading up to the outbreak of war.
D Day to VE Day: General Eisenhower's Report
General Eisenhower's personal account of the invasion of Europe, from June 1944 to May 1945.
The Judgment of Nuremberg, 1946
Focuses on the first trial of 21 major war criminals. The text describes the history, purpose and method of the Nazi party.

ISBN 0 11 702463 5   Price UK £14.99 US $19.95

The Siege Collection

The stories of four sieges involving British troops in the days
of British Empire are presented here.

The Siege of Kars, 1855

This little-known siege lasted five months and took place
during the Crimean War, in the mountains of eastern Turkey.

The Boer War: Ladysmith and Mafeking, 1900

Contains despatches describing the siege and relief of both
Ladysmith and Mafeking, as reported by the commanders in
the field. The reverses suffered at Spion Kop are included.

The Siege of the Peking Embassy, 1900

Tells the story of how the diplomatic staff in Peking, China,
were besieged by the Boxers in 1900, and how they were
rescued by an international force.

ISBN 0 11 702464 3   Price UK £14.99 US $19.95

Tragic Journeys

Features three of the most tragic journeys of the 20th century.

The Loss of the Titanic, 1912

The official inquiry presented here is the same report that was
published in 1912. Also included is a reappraisal of the
evidence relating to the SS *Californian*, the ship that failed to
come to the rescue of the *Titanic*.

R.101: The Airship Disaster, 1930

In its heyday, the airship R.101 was considered as glamorous as
the *Titanic*. Sadly, its fate was equally tragic, as she crashed on her
maiden flight to India. The official inquiry investigates why it
all went so disastrously wrong.

The Munich Air Crash, 1958

Eight key players from the Manchester United football team
died in this tragic accident at Munich airport in 1958.
Included here are the official inquiries into the causes.

ISBN 0 11 702465 1   Price UK £14.99 US $19.95

The War Facsimiles

The War Facsimiles are exact reproductions of illustrated books that were published during the war years. They were produced by the British government to inform people about the progress of the war and the home-defence operations.

The Battle of Britain, August–October 1940

On 8 August 1940, the Germans launched the first of a series of mass air attacks on Britain in broad daylight. For almost three months, British and German aircraft were locked in fierce and prolonged combat in what has become known as the Battle of Britain. In 1941 the government published *The Battle of Britain* to explain the strategy and tactics behind the fighting that had taken place high in the sky over London and south-east England. Such was the public interest in this document, with its graphic maps and photographs, that sales had reached two million by the end of the war.

ISBN 0 11 702536 4 Price UK £4.99 US $8.95

The Battle of Egypt, 1942

Often referred to as the Battle of El Alamein, this battle was one of the major turning points for the Allies in World War II. The British, commanded by General Montgomery, were defending Egypt while the Germans under Rommel were attacking. This was a campaign the British could not afford to lose, because not only would it leave Egypt wide open for invasion, but it would also mean the loss of the Suez Canal and the oil fields. First published in 1943, *The Battle of Egypt* is an astonishing contemporary report of one of the most famous military victories in British history.

ISBN 0 11 702542 9 Price UK £5.99 US $10.95

Bomber Command: the Air Ministry account of Bomber Command's offensive against the Axis, September 1939–July 1941

Churchill declared on 22 June 1941: "We shall bomb Germany by day as well as by night in ever-increasing measure." Bomber Command of the RAF was to translate those words into action, beginning its attacks on Germany in May 1940, and steadily increasing its efforts as the war progressed. Published in 1941 at the height of World War II, *Bomber Command* tells the story of this fighting force during those early years.

ISBN 0 11 702540 2   Price UK £5.99   US $11.95

East of Malta, West of Suez: the Admiralty account of the naval war in the eastern Mediterranean, September 1939 to March 1941

This is the story of the British Navy in action in the eastern Mediterranean from September 1939 to March 1941 and their bid to seize control. During this time British supremacy was vigorously asserted at Taranto and Matapan. This facsimile edition contains contemporary maps, air reconnaissance photographs of the fleets and photographs of them in action.

ISBN 0 11 702538 0   Price UK £4.99   US $8.95

Fleet Air Arm: the Admiralty account of naval air operations, 1943

The Fleet Air Arm was established in 1939 as the Royal Navy's own flying branch. With its vast aircraft carriers bearing squadrons of fighter pilots, its main role was to protect a fleet or convoy from attack, or to escort an air striking force into battle. In *Fleet Air Arm*, published in 1943, the public could read for the first time of the expeditions of these great ships as they pursued and sank enemy warships such as the *Bismarck*.

ISBN 0 11 702539 9   Price UK £5.99   US $11.95

Land at War: the official story of British farming 1939–1944

Land at War was published by the Ministry of Information in 1945 as a tribute to those who had contributed to the war effort at home. It explains how 300,000 farms, pinpointed by an extensive farm survey, had been expected to increase their production dramatically, putting an extra 6.5 million acres of grassland under the plough. This is a book not just about rural life, but of the determination of a people to survive the rigours of war.

ISBN 0 11 702537 2   Price UK £5.99   US $11.95

Ocean Front: the story of the war in the Pacific, 1941–44

Ocean Front tells the story of the Allies' war against Japan in the central and western Pacific. Starting with Pearl Harbor in December 1941, this fascinating book recounts the Allies' counter-offensive, from the battles of the Coral Sea and Midway, to the recapture of the Aleutian Islands and the final invasion of the Philippines. Illustrated throughout with amazing photographs of land and sea warfare, *Ocean Front* provides a unique record of the American, Australian and New Zealand fighting forces in action.

ISBN 0 11 702543 7   Price UK £5.99   US $11.95

Roof over Britain: the official story of Britain's anti-aircraft defences, 1939–1942

Largely untold, *Roof over Britain* is the story of Britain's ground defences against the attacks of the German air force during the Battle of Britain in the autumn of 1940. First published in 1943, it describes how the static defences – the AA guns, searchlights and balloons – were organised, manned and supplied in order to support the work of the RAF.

ISBN 0 11 702541 0   Price UK £5.99   US $11.95

Other titles in the series

Rillington Place

" 'I want to give myself up. I have disposed of my wife.' 'What do you mean?' said the constable. Evans replied 'I put her down the drain.' The officer told Evans to think again before he said any more, and Evans said 'I know what I am saying. I cannot sleep and I want to get it off my chest.' "

Backdrop
The serial killer, or mass murderer, is often seen as a creation of modern society, but quiet killers, drawing no attention to themselves in the teeming streets of the metropolis, have been responsible for some of the most notorious crimes of the 20th century.

The Book
On 9th March 1950, Timothy Evans, of 10 Rillington Place, London, was hanged for the murder of his daughter Geraldine. His wife Beryl had also been murdered at the same time. Three years later, Reginald Christie, also of the same address, was hanged for the murder of his wife, Ethel. In the course of the investigation, five more bodies were discovered at 10 Rillington Place. Since then, doubts have been raised over the conviction of Timothy Evans. This government inquiry by Lord Brabin is an attempt to uncover the truth surrounding those macabre events that took place in 1949.

ISBN 0 11 702417 1   Price UK £6.99   US $12.95

Escape from Germany, 1939–45

"It is quite certain that, apart from the microphone, no evidence whatever had been found to show a tunnel was being dug, yet in the four-and-a-half months from the commencement of the tunnel campaign, more than 166 tons of sand had been excavated from three tunnels and hidden in a compound only a mile in circumference which was constantly patrolled and inspected by Germans."

Backdrop

The history of Air Force captivity in Germany began on 3 September 1939, the day Britain declared war on Germany. On the same day, a New Zealand officer was shot down over the North Sea and was subsequently taken prisoner. By December 1939, the numbers of those captured had grown, and the Germans began to segregate Air Force prisoners, housing them in special camps.

The Book

Of the 10,000 British airmen held as prisoners-of-war by the Germans during World War II, less than 30 successfully managed to find their way back to Britain or to a neutral country. After 1945, many escapers and PoWs were interviewed, and a file was built up of their various experiences. This file was kept secret for nearly 40 years (despite the fact that several famous films were made about these escapes), as it was thought to contain evidence of enterprise and resilience that could still be useful to an enemy. Now "uncovered" for the public to read, this book contains the true and often incredible stories of the heroic attempts of these men to escape.

ISBN 0 11 702459 7   Price UK £6.99   US $14.95

King Guezo of Dahomey, 1850–51

"Retiring to our seats, the King insisted on our viewing the place of sacri-
fice. Immediately under the royal canopy were six or eight executioners,
armed with large knives, grinning horribly; the mob now armed with clubs
and branches, yelled furiously, calling upon the King to 'feed them – they
were hungry' ... When it was all over, at 3 pm, we were permitted to
retire. At the foot of the ladder in the boats and baskets lay the bleeding
heads. It is my duty to describe; I leave exposition to the reader."

Backdrop
In 1807, the British Parliament outlawed the trade in slaves,
followed in 1833 by an Act to abolish the institution of slavery.
However, in 1850, the slave trade was alive and well on the
west coast of Africa.

The Book
The fact that Africans were still being sold into slavery in the
mid-19th century was partly due to the reluctance of both the
merchants and the African chiefs to desist. King Guezo was one
of these African chiefs who profited by selling captives taken
during tribal wars. Although he was very friendly towards the
British, counting Queen Victoria as one of his most revered
friends, he was reluctant to give up his war-like habits. With
18,000 royal wives, an army composed in part of 3,000
Amazon women, and a warrior-like reputation to maintain, he
could see little attraction in farming as an alternative lifestyle.

Lord Palmerston was the Foreign Secretary who charged the
British Consul in west Africa with the unenviable task of per-
suading the African chiefs to give up their lucrative trade. Just
how the British managed to coerce the chiefs into abandoning
this practice is revealed in fresh and fascinating detail by these
contemporary despatches. They provide an astonishing glimpse
of the customs and way of life in Africa some 150 years ago.

ISBN 0 11 702460 0   Price UK £6.99   US $12.95

The Irish Uprising, 1914–21: Papers from the British Parliamentary Archive

Backdrop
In 1914 it was still the case that the whole of Ireland was part of Great Britain, under the dominion of the King, and Irish constituencies were represented in the British Parliament.

The Book
This book contains five remarkable documents published by the British Government between 1914 and 1921, relating to the events leading up to the partition of Ireland in 1921. In the first, a report is made into the shooting of civilians following a landing of arms at Howth outside Dublin. The second is of the papers discovered relating to the activities of Sinn Fein and particularly of Sir Roger Casement. The third is the government inquiry into the Easter Rising of 1916. The fourth describes the treatment of three journalists by the British Army shortly after the uprising, and the last is an exchange of correspondence between Eamon de Valera and David Lloyd George prior to the Anglo-Irish Treaty of 1921.

ISBN 0 11 702415 5   Price UK £6.99   US $12.95

Uncovered editions: how to order

FOR CUSTOMERS IN THE UK

Ordering is easy. Simply follow one of these five ways:

Online

Visit www.clicktso.com

By telephone

Please call 0870 600 5522, with book details to hand.

By fax

Fax details of the books you wish to order (title, ISBN, quantity and price) to: 0870 600 5533.

Please include details of your credit/debit card plus expiry date, your name and address and telephone number, and expect a handling charge of £3.00.

By post

Post the details listed above (under 'By fax') to:

The Stationery Office

PO Box 29

Norwich NR3 1GN

You can send a cheque if you prefer by this method (made payable to The Stationery Office). Please include a handling charge of £3 on the final amount.

TSO bookshops

Visit your local TSO bookshop (or any good bookshop).

FOR CUSTOMERS IN THE UNITED STATES

Uncovered editions are available through all major wholesalers and bookstores, and are distributed to the trade by Midpoint Trade Books.

Phone 913 831 2233 for single copy prepaid orders which can be fulfilled on the spot, or simply for more information.

Fax 913 362 7401